THE DEATH OF
SARDANAPALUS

And they are smart —
that's how they found you . . .

THE DEATH OF SARDANAPALUS will shake the dreamers awake and call the dog soldiers from the complacency of their corporate graves. "To a Child of Baghdad" should be reprinted again and again, on every website, in every magazine and every newspaper. It is the definitive work—the master work—of defiance against the neo-Cons, neo-Nazis, and an illegal war destined to last 50 years or more. This is a clarion call to storm the Bastille. It inspired me to paint my face and poison my arrows.   —*Gregory Greyhawk*

There are some breathers, pools of meditative almost-calm in David Ray's *THE DEATH OF SARDANAPALUS,* notably when we reach his sequence for conscientious objector William Stafford, but his primary voice is that of jaw-clenched ironic rage as he tries to teach his heart not to love—as a critic wisely said of Robinson Jeffers. This is a relentless book infused with more enlightenment than the author gives himself credit for, a book that knows we have chosen the barbarians within ourselves as our masters. Indeed, in deed, after such knowledge, what forgiveness?--only the dispensations of powerful and necessary poetry, as here. —*William Heyen*

In these times of an imperialist upsurge and religious wars, we need stories and songs of vision to nourish us and give us strength to carry on in the world. We need truth tellers like David Ray, who keeps his eyes, ears and heart open during the destruction, and witnesses in these poems with a heartbreaking eloquence.
—*Joy Harjo*

THE DEATH OF SARDANAPALUS is relentless and devastating. It illuminates what poetry can truly do and say as Goya showed what art could portray in his "Disasters of War" and "Saturn Devouring His Children." David Ray's colossal anti-war tome is a major milestone, a visionary blessing that proves once and for all poetry's power and grace. These are the kind of poems that help save the world. *SARDANAPALUS is exquisitely beautiful!* —*Antler*

Very few poets give one such an authentic sense of lived life as David Ray; and he can be intensely personal without indulging in narcissism. ... these poems are not versified travel-reports: all is seen through the individual lens of Ray's acute consciousness of the terrors and anguish of current history. And his own abiding grief, the unassuageable grief of a bereaved father, does not prevent him from perceiving great beauty in the world or from knowing (and giving to the reader) moments of grace and blessing. —*Denise Levertov*

David Ray is one of the best and most powerful writers I know. He brings ferocious intelligence to his work. Considering the burden of pain he labors under, it's remarkable that he's as productive and as clear as he manages to consistently be. ... What's special about David's work is that he remembers so clearly and with such honesty. —*Richard Rhodes*

BRAVE NEW WORLD ORDER BOOKS
DESIGNED & EDITED BY MICHAEL ANNIS
WWW.HOWLINGDOGPRESS.COM

The Sun goes down: methinks he sets more slowly,
Taking his last look of Assyria's Empire.
How red he glares amongst those deepening clouds,
Like the blood he predicts. If not in vain,
Thou Sun that sinkest, and ye stars which rise,
I have outwatched ye, reading ray by ray
The edicts of your orbs, which make Time tremble
For what he brings the nations, 'tis the furthest
Hour of Assyria's years. And yet how calm!
An earthquake should announce so great a fall —
A summer's sun discloses it. Yon disk,
To the star-read Chaldean, bears upon
Its everlasting page the end of what
Seemed everlasting; but oh! thou true Sun!
The burning oracle of all that live,
As fountain of all life, and symbol of
Him who bestows it, wherefore dost thou limit
Thy lore unto calamity? Why not
Unfold the rise of days more worthy thine
All-glorious burst from ocean? Why not dart
A beam of hope athwart the future years,
As of wrath to its days? Hear me! oh, hear me!
I am thy worshipper, thy priest, thy servant —
I have gazed on thee at thy rise and fall,
And bowed my head beneath thy mid-day beams,
When my eye dared not meet thee. I have watched
For thee, and after thee, and prayed to thee,
And sacrificed to thee, and read, and feared thee,
And asked of thee, and thou hast answered — but
Only to thus much: while I speak, he sinks —
Is gone — and leaves his beauty, not his knowledge,
To the delighted West, which revels in
Its hues of dying glory. Yet what is
Death, so it be but glorious? 'Tis a sunset;
And mortals may be happy to resemble
The Gods but in decay.

—from SARDANAPALUS, *by* George Gordon, Lord Byron

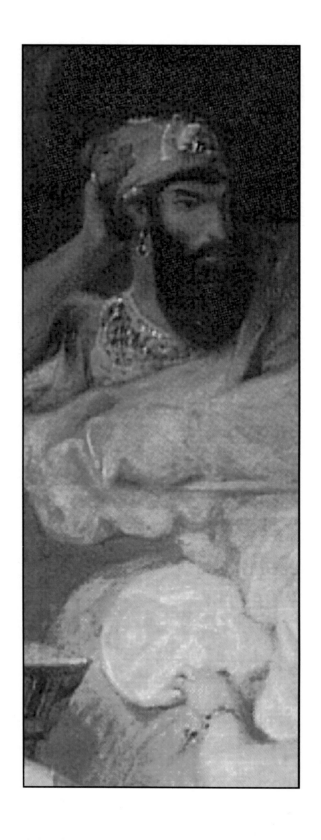

THE DE**A**TH OF
SARDANAPALUS

AND OTHER POEMS
OF THE IRAQ WARS

by

DAVID RAY

HOWLING DOG PRESS
BRAVE NEW WORLD ORDER BOOKS

THE DEATH OF SARDANAPALUS
AND OTHER POEMS OF THE IRAQ WARS

COPYRIGHT © 2004 BY DAVID RAY

ACKNOWLEDGEMENTS

Howling Dog Press would like to thank Michael Romoth for his artistic composition *Sardanapalus in Guernica,* and Judy Ray for superior, last minute copy-editing. The author and publisher are grateful to Lilvia Soto for all Spanish translations of poems included in this book, and to David McCann and Diana Evans of Harvard University for help with the Korean poetry. Some of the poems in this collection (many in variant versions) have previously appeared in the following publications:

MAGAZINES AND NEWSPAPERS:
Another Chicago Magazine; Chariton Review; Chelsea; Crooked Roads; Friends Bulletin; Greenfield Review; The Himalayan Times (Nepal); *The Human Quest; New Letters; Potpourri; Re-Markings* (India); *River King; Rosebud; The Same; SandStar's Poetry for Peace; Southern California Anthology; TIWA;* and *Westerly* (Australia).

ANTHOLOGIES AND COLLECTIONS:
One Thousand Years: Poems About the Holocaust; Kangaroo Paws; Out of This World; Poets Against the War; Poetry of Peace; September 11, 2001: American Writers Respond. "Flying Over Cheyenne Mountain" won the 2001 Nuclear Age Peace Foundation Poetry Award.

ONLINE:
The Death of Sardanapalus (e-chapbook) at www.HowlingDogPress.com/Sardanapalus; *OMEGA* [www.HowlingDogPress.com/OMEGA] *XRAYS* [www.HowlingDogPress.com/Xrays]; *Melnicreview.com; Poetsagainstthewar.org; Voicesinwartime.org.*

LIBRARY OF CONGRESS CATALOGING-IN-PUBLICATION DATA

Ray, David, 1932 —
    The Death of Sardanapalus: Poems of the Iraq Wars / David Ray.
      p.   cm.

    ISBN 1-882863-55-0 (paper)

[CATALOGING APPLIED FOR AND PENDING]
CIP

THE ENDSHEETS artwork of the catastrophic aftermath of the September 11, 2001, devastation of the World Trade Center, NYC, is presented in this book as a supreme irony, since neither the publisher nor the author recognize any connection whatsoever of that event to the former government of Saddam Hussein, and the ensuing imperialist invasion of the sovereign country of Iraq by the Bush administration as it continues to maintain and promote the fallacious assertion that there is — however subtle, innuendoed, or clandestine be their propaganda.

*This book is dedicated to all who speak out against war
and to those who encourage dissent and artistic expression
rather than crush unwelcome voices
with every manner of censorship official and covert.*

*To speak out is to recover true freedom, always at hazard,
but we who cannot remain silent are fired with a sense
of urgency, hoping that our words may matter for more
than the processing of grief and sorting through rubble.*

*And thus, this book is also dedicated
to the reader.*

*A most special thanks
to poet and publisher Michael Annis
for his interactive empowerment and far more.
We unite in dedicating this book to our lost sons,*

Samuel *and* Dylan,

*and the peaceful world they would have worked for
had they lived to inherit it.*

THE DEATH OF SARDANAPALUS

YET ANOTHER WAR: A Sequence for William Stafford

We soldiers of all nations who lie killed
Ask little: that you never, in our name,
Dare claim we died that men might be fulfilled.
The earth should vomit us, against that shame.

— James Agee

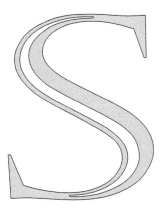

THE BLACK HOLE ▲▼▲

*"The discovery indicates, the astronomers assert, that
they have seen energy pouring out of a black hole and
into the surrounding universe for the first time."*
—*The New York Times,*
October 22, 2001

Though the news is of interest
to the rest of the cosmos

as well as to earth
we did not need the astronomers

to tell us that out of a black hole
glows far more than what

poured into it. Out of that
gaping ground zero in Manhattan

has flashed into outer space
even to distant galaxies more grief

than earthly equation can measure.
And in the spectrum of distant light

glowing beyond human reach
can be discerned even without telescopes

all that was poured into the hole —
love beyond measure, sorrow

in its every manifestation,
and the anger that is allowed even in heaven.

THE ESCAPEES ▲▼▲

all those serfs singing
all those nuns mumbling
all those dervish dancers
all those battered survivors
holding out in the ruins

and now these lost ones
dissolved into a day
otherwise perfect.
these are the voices
still chanting — hear them

in the wind or where
they tell you in dreams
what you too must know
though all other teachings
must be banished. who

is to say their voices
have been silenced?
what else is keeping you
awake? whose are the faces
in dreams if not theirs?

and where are you also
afloat in the minds
of others, and still
to undergo the passage
of time into eternity?

CLAIRVOYANCE ▲▼▲

"Elizabeth Newport frequently exhibited what can be
properly called clairvoyance, in which she was able to
discern the future or to reveal conditions within a person
not known to any but themselves."
        —Memoir compiled by Ann A. Townsend, 1878

Do I believe my friend Miles when he relates
his dream — the one interrupted
by his wife's call to come look at the news,
just in time to see the second plane
hit the tower and the flames roiling away,
grey smoke shrouding some of it — the death
within? As the towers collapsed
Miles and Mary stood in their living room
and saw a few victims leaping out windows
before the TV producers decided
       This is too much, even for us.

Damn right I believe him — Miles
my friend and tai chi teacher and vet
of Vietnam. In the dream he had stood
high in a skyscraper, peering out through
a window taped in black except for a slot
like that in a tank or a helmet. He gazed
down upon both towers and the Empire
State Building. And although he knew
even in the dream that the perspective
was all wrong, he thought nothing of it.
Next to him two men were chatting —
       "young middle-eastern men."

Although they were not speaking in English,
Miles is still trying to recover what
they said just before he awoke to see
what the rest of us saw — he and his wife
in their living room, I and my wife
standing in ours as we said: this must

be a movie, not the news. It's just
a mix-up on Channel Four — but also
on Nine and Thirteen. We did not
check *Sesame Street* as we began to weep.

My friend Miles would never lie
and I've had enough odd events in my life
to know they can happen — the clairvoyant,
the telepathic, the never explainable.
Death opens the door for such glimpses
into other worlds. But soon such a witness
as Miles betrays the gift he has been given,
begins to apologize, says "You must think
I am nuts." They work hard to convince
themselves that the dream was only a dream,
nothing more. But the nightmare is what
              they awake to, not what they dream.

RAINING RICE, RAINING ASH ᴬᵛᴬ

"a blizzard of hard rice
Sliding by, sliding by, polished smooth as the stone
Each of us thinks he is standing on ..."
      —Patricia Goedicke

Solid enough under our feet were the corridors,
even the floors of elevators. We were accustomed
to the sensation of plunging as if by parachute
and were fond of the ascent so smooth we could read
between floors, skipping a vast number. We were sure
we would arrive in the sky on schedule, but not too high
for such pleasures as we enjoyed on *terra firma.*

There was not much missing, for love now and then
broke out as a bonus. Our eyrie was indeed the last place
we might expect hell's fire to reach, nor would we
in a thousand years rename it Armageddon or the Inferno.
Sometimes flowers grew as effusive as heaven's
or those in gardens deemed safe in suburbs
or recalled from a land where we wandered as tourists.
Bouquets would appear on a desk for the least success,
the blessed largesse of blossoms.

Even here, in our precinct of work and play, clouds
drifted by — often below, not above us. Rivulets of rain
ran down the windows or fog closed in though pavements
below remained dry. Before we left for a luncheon
a taxi distance away we would telephone down to ground
to ask if we would need umbrellas. Now so much
has been condensed into anecdote, survivors sorted
into categories, value of lost loves quantified,
that only God could recover a last moment, a final
word in flight, or cubit of that day's virginal blue sky
to place on the scale. A few saw a plane homing in,
even face of the pilot, could only report it a second

or less before widows became widows, obliged
to prove what their husbands were worth.

Fate is paper, numbers, and nomenclature. Therefore,
woe to the unmarried and to lovers illicit
or lesbian, gay or merely engaged. To hell
with papers due to be signed on September the twelfth.
Woe to women whose wails join the winds and to men
who weep for the first time. Woe for the words
not to come to fill the abyss that once reached the sky
as I grieve a hollow bronze torso and foot in the ash,
                         signed A. Rodin.

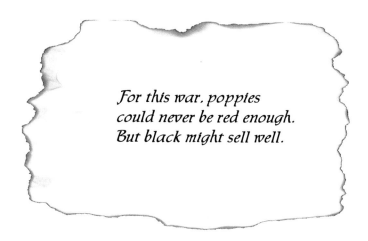

For this war, poppies
could never be red enough.
But black might sell well.

PREPARING THE MONUMENT ▵▿▵

They are hard at work on a monument
while the smoke is still roiling out of the pit,

raising the question of how much effort
It takes to pound the present into the past

and quickly convert a disaster still in progress
to the status of an ancient and archaic attraction.

They have chosen a fire truck mangled and twisted
to set on a plinth, along with a few smashed cars.

They are extracting relics not yet gone cold
and unearthing what is already entombed.

Though the dust has not settled and the smoke
is still noxious in nostrils they are braving

fouled air to assemble debris, and have applied
for permission to choose an unknown victim

to be interred in salvaged aluminum. For any
design calling for names stamped in bricks, tiles,

frieze or entablature they have been given a list.
Once their monument, centered on a smooth terrace

with a few tasteful trees, is in place they can gaze
upon this space called ground zero and not be blinded

or overcome by the stench, and when their work
is complete and every surface polished and gleaming

and ready for tourists, they themselves will be free
of fear, as if they are dealing only with the archaic —

desiccate, bloodless, and cold, with no smoke
in the air, and no catastrophe in progress. Once

I too sought out the archaic and found it on an island
in Greece, a fragment in marble that had once

been the foot of a lion, but he was already a thing
of the past and I did not have to chase him there.

As for the present, Buddha said it well —
everything is burning — everything —

and to enshrine the flames is hardly a task
for mere mortals.

THE PANIC AFTER 9-11 ▲▼▲

"Though the people of the world have mouths
full of deceit, and changeable words, yet
I was to keep to Yea and Nay in all things."
— George Fox

Every suitcase a bomb.
Every rental truck full of explosives.
Every intaken breath anthrax
unless it is smallpox revived,

smallpox — which we once had
the chance to destroy — the last
of the microbes, in a petri dish.
It was kept to develop a vaccine

or in case an enemy somehow
also acquired it. Tell me another!
What government would rid
the world of a plague when

it might someday be a weapon?
Every suitcase a bomb, every set
of moving lips those of a liar.
I have an entomologist friend

who claims there's a species of ants
more vicious than man. Tell me another.
Even when I gave up telling lies
I never renounced my intention to deceive.

DIVIDED WE STAND ▲▼▲

The attack on September eleventh was not,
it seems, the first time ground zero was bombed,
although the first was by wrecking cranes,
not jet planes, and the war was between builders
and those defending the charm and vitality
of Lower Manhattan, the historic fishing village
that had become Radio Row, great for shopping.
Many had homes there, and were chased away
lest they lie down and die in dust and debris.

Defenders fought in vain. Robert Moses —
Czar, Pope, and King of Traffic — exulted cars
above people, destroyed many neighborhoods,
razed homes as if they were in conquered lands.
Expressways were to lead straight from Lower
Manhattan to Heaven. He could turn any acre
to rubble. In vain did a man declare that "they
can't do this to us. This is America, not Russia."

No one could defeat the millionaire brothers —
David with his dream, Nelson as Governor.
To justify eminent domain, he decreed
a "public purpose," and the wrecking ball swung
madly for months —"a ferocious land grab,"
"a fever of destruction," "a martyrdom of buildings."
Cranes and bulldozers did the work of bombs,
though souls did not fly out high windows
with dust, ash, and blood as in the later attacks.

"World capitalism is a great church like the Vatican,"
David Rockefeller proclaimed, and his towers

went up as assertion, defiance, exultation, targets.
Thus September eleventh was not the first battle,
only the most horrid so far — more damage inflicted
in minutes than some armies manage in a long war.
The smoldering ruins, like censers in a cathedral,
give off smoke of incense we inhale as communion.

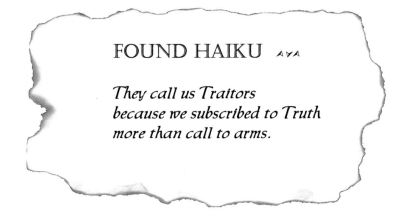

FOUND HAIKU ▲▼▲

They call us Traitors
because we subscribed to Truth
more than call to arms.

TERRORISM ᴀʏᴀ

The roving reporter asks
"How do you feel about it,
terrorism and all that?"

"It has not yet permeated
my lifestyle," says a skin
care lady in Denver, found

waiting for a plane. "I guess
if they blow us up they'll just
blow us up, but so what?"

Maybe that's the right attitude
is my thought. Another inter-
viewee, a young mother

encountered in San Francisco,
says "I don't want to be across
any bridge if it happens."

That too seems an admirable
attitude. Then she adds:
"It scares me just to think

my baby may be all the way
across the bay when it happens."
The threat varies day by day

we are told. The Brooklyn
Bridge is at risk one day,

the Golden Gate the next.

Reactions vary greatly
but Angst and Fear prevail
at least until the election.

LEFTOVER WARS CAN STILL BE WARMED UP ᴧᴠᴧ

I can't shake this image of McNamara
at the White House breakfast
passing on with a smile his stale war,
warmed up as if in a microwave.

WRITTEN BEFORE
THE 48-HOUR ULTIMATUM ᴀᴠᴀ

Although I know it is naïve, perverse, and infantile,
I cannot stop thinking of the children of Baghdad
who will soon be dealt with as if they are no more
than dust of the street, clay figurines to be shattered.

After all, it's for a grand cause — Peace! So why
should I feel sad about them, gone to that good cause?
Would they not want their little lives to stand
for something admirable and of lasting value?

Besides, are they not all children of Saddam?
Moreover, we need such concern as we have
back here at home where there is far too much
murder and pedophilia. That's an odd term, I know,

since it means love of little tykes, and it is hardly love
to violate them. Or so you might think. But is that
not splitting hairs, this semantics and semiotics stuff?
With language we must be flexible, inventive,

even tricky, and when push comes to shove we can
take comfort in knowing there are no realities,
only perceptions, as is now taught in the academies.
A child is blown off the map, a mere perception!

Otherwise we could hardly pull off a sentence,
much less a war. In any case, taking out little tykes
and grownups as well is nothing gross like pedophilia.
It's a clean shot — missiles are not nearly as messy

as bombs used to be. There has been much improvement
since World War II and Vietnam. We must also recall

that fate is involved, and fate we should not interfere with.
Karma is sacred, be it that of an Iraqi or a tyke from Colorado.

Little Jon-Benet the strip tease artist and beauty queen
was raped and strangled, but she would surely have preferred
to be bombed — though not by Mommy and/or Daddy. Bottom
line is that we must not fret about children, what happens

to them when bombers fly over or tanks rumble in. The old-
fashioned concept of sin does not even apply. You have not
heard Billy Graham lamenting the fate of the children
of Baghdad, the sins of whose fathers are visited upon them.

In truth, the vaporized have no hope of heaven.

FLYING OVER
CHEYENNE MOUNTAIN ᴧʏᴧ

> *"The reflection that for the first time in history the*
> *phenomenon of a great city, like New York, being there*
> *in the morning and not being there in the afternoon could*
> *perfectly well occur."*
>
> — James Gould Cozzens

You gaze down on the snow-capped mountains
unchanged since John Muir beheld them,

but you do not know which is hollowed out
for gnomes to enact their Wagnerian opera,

some cities gone to the boom of kettle drums,
others to oboes and firestorms, violins so vibrato

that earth will shake as ash overtakes distant suburbs
and men become writhing flesh, no better than

earthworms tormented. It is the hour we fear
we will come to, when the maestro's fulfillment

will lie in conducting the final performance,
so explosive that the audience will be consumed

in the adoration. But has this climax long planned
not been devoutly wished, as if it is our first cosmic

feat sure to be seen from other galaxies?
Until they fall, all the mountains are holy save one.

SESTINA FOR A TROUBLED YEAR ᴧᵥᴧ

"The beast of dialectic dragged his chains"
— Stanley Kunitz

Our hosts of the evening both believe in the war,
how we must have it, and how evil by good
must be put in its place. If there have been lies
in abundance they have been told for good reason.
The worst weapons, whether found or not, must exist,
for our leader says so, and all has been decided.

There is nothing that has not already been decided.
There is no point in debating, for we are going to war.
It is sad, but those in the way have no right to exist.
They must be destroyed, but only for the greater good.
And we guests who sit at dinner should not try to reason
with those who have accepted as gospel all the lies.

In our lives we have learned not to challenge most lies,
for they too often prevail when any issue is decided
and it's a convention to lie if it's for the right reason.
Propaganda well used is a tool to inspire such a war,
for the public may not be aware of the greater good
that cannot be stated, for fear it cannot be proved to exist.

Those in power will decide who has a right to exist
and what cities will fall into rubble as a result of the lies
though we must recall that this war is for the greater good,
when the most terrible weapons will be unleashed as decided.
Don't forget that peace — only peace — is the goal of this war
and if you do not understand that, you are deficient in reason.

I confess I am stupid, for I cannot grasp the reason
we must bomb foreign lands — perhaps for oil that is said to exist
by billions of barrels under the sands, well worth a war.
And yet I am bothered by some of the most obvious lies,
and I still find it odd that one man in power has decided
for all the world that this war is defined as the great good.

He has never been in a war, so how can he know it is good
when the killing begins and men seem to have lost all reason
until the hell they have made relents and an outcome's decided.
As they kill and are killed they will fight for one goal — to exist —
and before it is over many will hate all the lies
and those who have told them to bring on the war.

I never saw a good war. I do not think a war can be good.
Each starts and ends with lies, excuses, and some reason
to use weapons that exist, the how, why, and where by fools decided.

SIX MONTHS AFTER ▲▼▲

This is what it means
to understand history —
Tolstoy: *We never go*
back far enough, just
credit the latest Napoleon
with all the damage.

Walter Benjamin:
one single catastrophe
which keeps piling up
wreckage...the pile
of debris growing
skyward.

"We all see a piece
of history," said Tony
the fireman, no longer
a boy on probation.
"It was raining bodies,"
said another, holding
an axe. "I found
a foot encased
in the rubble."

This man with an axe
and a helmet rubbed tears
from his eyes, and that
is what it means
to understand history,
although there is also
the scream and the shriek,
the drumbeat of bodies

striking the roof.

SANDHILL CRANES
CIRCLING THEIR TARGETS

These high-flying cranes are not
warplanes filling the winter sky,
nor can they manage to outnumber
the thousands of bombers
heading out over the seas, sent
to throw fear with each shadow —
terror for terror — real or imagined.

These wings are gentler. The eyes
are not so merciless as those of pilots,
nor have they been trained to leave
devastation in their wake — the rubble
of cities, the bodies dismembered.

At worst these cranes have raided
fields of grain, lived off the land.
High above us they glitter at one
moment, then disappear, invisible
to hunters and hawks. But children
beneath bombers have not these abilities.

When the sun strikes wings of these
wheeling wonders it is as if the sky
is filled with confetti. Thousands
of cranes have woven and braided
their strings of glitter, reminding me
of Rockefeller Center at Christmas
as skaters swoop and glide in similar
glissandos — but on far thicker ice
than that of our president's policies.

Our leader says the war will be swift
and short, a sure victory. He sounds

like Alcibiades addressing the Athenians,
convincing them to set out in their triremes.
Thus to learn about war you look to Thucydides,
not to the spin masters of Washington.

This year I suggest we swap bombers
and fighters for cranes — one for one —
until we have the most impressive fleet
                                    in the world.

In Texas he killed
with a smile, mocking those souls
who begged from death row.

ROUTINE ▲▼▲

Global or local, it's always
fair weather for armaments.
Schoolboy gunmen go
on a killing spree, turn

school into an abattoir,
and in sight of the Capitol
snipers kill at will and at random.
But as the heads of victims

are not impaled on poles along
with flags and the bloody bodies
are not laid out on the floors
of both Senate and House

gun control is again voted down,
and the gentlemen give the same
oft-stated reasons. Also, their own
children are grown and no one

of late has murdered a president.
And therefore, "However many
it takes!" is the price they are still
willing to pay to bow to the will

of the N.R.A. And as the heads
from Iraq and Afghanistan are not
brought back and rolled down
the aisles and because children

of those with the power to make war
are not among troops in harm's way
we can safely say that "However
many it takes!" tells us how many
must die to bow to the president's will.

THE PHENOMENON ▲▼▲

It is a phenomenon George Grosz
the artist noticed many times —

how men and women would
turn into pigs before his very eyes.

You can see it in his paintings,
how gross and evil they became.

When I first saw this strange thing
happen — though not in Nazi Germany —

I was amazed, for I was just a toddler.
Later, when such a sight was nothing

new, I felt myself a fool. Why did I
never learn, I asked, for it had happened

more than once. As children we
would point, though reprimanded often.

We would ask if what we saw was true.
Had a man — perhaps a father or a neighbor

or an uncle back from war — really turned
into a pig? Children tell the truth

and thus we always answered yes.
We smelled the smell. We heard the squeal.

Hitler squealed and millions heard it not.
And now another mounts the podium

and the child in me cries out and points,
but no one else seems to find it strange

that public men should be applauded for their squeals.

Some lie sleeping, unaware
they may be next, that no
beginning stays at the beginning.

OUT OF THE FIFTIES ▲▼▲

"The horror is that there is no horror."
Alexander Kuprin

Panic's the subject as a friend speaks
of his mother — a volunteer plane spotter
back in the fifties. She once noticed

a gleaming jet trail stabbing the sky
at great height and parabolic velocity,
then ran in and called the White House,

demanded to speak to Ike himself,
the President. Then she threw down
the phone and went running through town —

like Henny Penny, her son said —
shouting warnings, pointing up
to the sky. She rounded up children,

led them down under a bridge
where they huddled while she told
Sunday school stories, trying to make

Armageddon sound bearable.

LOS GUERREROS ▲▼▲

"A los jóvenes declarados culpables de no registrarse
para la leva se les puede imponer una multa de hasta
$250,000, condenar a prisión por un período de hasta
cinco años, o ambos castigos."
        —Folleto del Selective Service System

¡Oh, cómo me gustaría ser jenízaro!
Dicen que era un placer —
como puedes ver
en las miniaturas enmarcadas —
cómo vestido de túnica de color pastel
con la cabeza envuelta
en una toalla o en un casco
como cáscara vacía
sales en una horda
de aquéllos con quienes estableces lazos
de hermano,
las pezuñas de tu caballo
levantan nubes de polvo
al avanzar,
invadir y conquistar,
todo para servir al Sultán —
Suleiman I,
quizá — o a su hijo
o al Fulano que sea
el jefe de turno. No
cabe duda que sería
fantástico ser tan valiente,
estar dispuesto a verter tu sangre
y ser diestro
con la espada
y otras armas disponibles
para lanzar cabezas en voleo alto
como pelotas de fútbol. ¡Oh,
hijo mío, qué no daría por ser
jenízaro! Pues dicen

THE WARRIORS ◣▾◢

*"Young men convicted of failure to register [for
the draft] may be fined up to $250,000,
imprisoned for up to five years, or both."*
—Selective Service System brochure

Oh, to be a janissary!
They say it was a joy —
as you can see
in framed miniatures —
how pastel-robed
with head wrapped
in a towel or helmet
like a hollow shell
you ride out in a horde
of those you bond with
just like brothers,
your horse hooves
lofting clouds of dust
as you advance,
invade, and conquer,
all to serve the Sultan —
Suleiman the First,
perhaps — or his son
or Whoever Else
might be in charge. No
question it would be
great to be so fearless,
glad to give your blood
and good enough
at sword play and other
weaponry at hand
to lob heads high
as footballs. Oh,
my son, to be
a janissary! For

que era un vacilón.
En los colegios hoy en día
los que reclutan les venden ese gozo
a los chicos
y también a bastantes
Señoritas Jenízaras.

—Translated by Lilvia Soto

they say it was a hoot.
At high school now
recruiters sell the joy
to every boy
as well as quite a few
Miss Janissary girls.

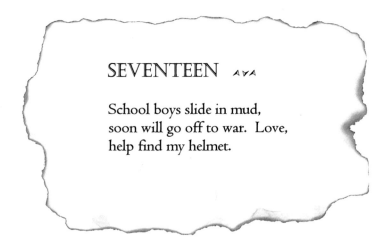

SEVENTEEN ⋏⋎⋏

School boys slide in mud,
soon will go off to war. Love,
help find my helmet.

CONGRESS ▲▼▲

A few good women
spoke up
and a few good men.

The others voted
Gung-ho for war.
And then gave more

billions every time
they were asked although
we cannot afford

such luxuries as
health care, clean air,
or voting machines

that will guarantee
an honest election —
the last thing desired

in our unique democracy.

COMBAT STRESS CONTROL ᴧ⌄ᴧ

The troops have been rehearsing for months
as if for a football game or a movie,

learning to act and speak their brave lines.
They practice injecting themselves

against nerve gas, and the psychiatrist
makes his rounds of the tents, checking up

on those who have threatened suicide
even before shock and awe is unleashed.

The doctor has a hundred memorized mutilation
jokes, a card deck for each patient, a DVD

player with lots of Elvis, and a mission.
He once said, "I joined up because

I was looking for a job where I could help
people." And that's what he is doing

with his pep talk to inspire men and women
to rush out and kill and be killed, after one

final rehearsal. They put on the gas masks
and proceed with the decontamination

of themselves from every threat but propaganda.

THE BATTLE OF
CROWHEART BUTTE ᴧᵥᴧ

— for Jim Corbett

Just before George Bush unleashed
the bombing attacks on Baghdad

called Shock and Awe, Saddam Hussein
was interviewed by Dan Rather on TV.

The Iraqi leader denied he had weapons
of mass destruction, invited Americans

to come into Iraq and search even more
diligently. And then he challenged Bush

to a debate. It would be televised all
over the world. Man to man they would try

to work out some alternative to what
clearly was coming. All this was in vain

since evil Saddam could not be trusted,
and so forth. George Bush could not

be lured into a debate, but when warriors
of the Shoshone and Crow tribes were formed

into battle lines Chief Washakie stepped forth
and raised his hands in a peace gesture.

"If we fight," he said, "many on both sides
will die. But if two chiefs fight only one

must die." On a high butte to assure that no
warriors intervened the two chiefs fought

and then the victor ate the loser's heart.
Perhaps it matters little which tribe won,

for what is important is that only one warrior died
and only one heart was sacrificed to the madness.

ON THE OUTBREAK OF WAR ᴀɣᴀ

She studies her garden like a scientist
bent to a microscope. "Look
at the ants," she says, "isn't it amazing,
how they never collide?"

We discuss electrons, busy bees,
lovers who don't see each other
for years, might pass in a crowd.
Now and then we catch a glimpse

of each other across a room or when
we wander the world of infinite
possibilities. Others run Olympics,
fight wars. We try to get by with

a maximum of silence, not to be
diverted from our play by grim adults.
We're never quite as frenetic as ants.
On that we can agree. Our products

are never as sweet as honey, or as sure
to survive as pollen. She puts down
her trowel, presses palm to waist
for support, stands up without breaking

bones. "The world is still too big
for us," she says, and I agree
that the years flowed by with deceptive
swift currents, bearing the corpses.

We discuss it — how as children
we thought the world was too big

to hug, then for a few years believed
it was manageable, embraceable.

Now we know again what we forgot.
Once more we are amazed at how much
killing the world can accommodate,
how even when we quit noticing

the earth was still breathing.

LOS RESTOS ⋏⋎⋏

¿Por qué parece más puro,
más digno de canto —

el dolor de los que
no han rescatado nada,

no han recuperado
ni un dedo de mano ni de pie,

los que deben aceptar el hecho bruto
del olvido, ni siquiera cenizas

para esparcir en su océano preferido?
Mientras que yo en mi galaxia de moléculas

giro por un día más,
sólo puedo preguntar qué importa —

de dónde partimos,
en qué dirección vamos,

el número de la ruta
y adónde nos llevan los vientos.

¿Volveremos
al punto de donde partimos,

en el corazón de una estrella?

—Translated by Lilvia Soto

THE REMAINS ᴧᵥᴧ

Why does it seem more pure,
more worthy of song —

the grief of those
who have salvaged nothing,

been able to retrieve
not so much as a finger or toe,

who must accept the brute fact
of oblivion, not even ash

to scatter upon the ocean of choice?
As I, in my galaxy of molecules,

whirl through another day
I can only ask what it matters —

whence we depart,
in what direction we go,

what number the route,
and whither the winds take us.

Will we not arrive back
where we set out,

in the heart of a star?

BUMERANGS ⋏⋎⋏

¿Has pensado mucho
últimamente en los bumerangs —

en cómo los tiras,
en cómo regresan,

a veces con mutaciones
sorprendentes, transformaciones,

e.g., las bombas que regresan
tan prolíficas como los dientes de dragón

aunque recuerdas haber lanzado
sólo una al cielo, viéndola

desaparecer en la distancia?
A menudo, dicen

del amor, recibes más
de lo que diste y de lo que esperabas —

regla que sirve
para bumerangs y bombas.

¿Quién ha jamás logrado lanzar
un bumerang llamado guerra

y que lo golpee en la cabeza
una bendición llamada paz?

—Translated by Lilvia Soto

BOOMERANGS

Have you thought much
about boomerangs lately —

how you throw them out,
how they return,

sometimes with surprising
mutations, transmogrifications,

e.g., bombs that come back
as prolific as dragon's teeth

though you recall flinging out
just one into the sky, watching

it disappear in the distance?
More often than not, they say

of love, you get back more
than you gave and bargained

for — a rule that holds true
for boomerangs and bombs.

Who ever succeeded in throwing
out a boomerang called war

and getting hit over the head
by a blessing called peace?

DOUBT ▲▼▲

"No Doubt that soldiers had to be marching
And that drums had to be rolling, rolling, rolling."
— Wallace Stevens

Oh, but there is doubt, a cloud of it
dark as a shroud floating around the world,

its shadow falling upon one land after another.
There is doubt that this war need ever

have been born, and doubt that it will ever die,
and doubt that its instigators foresee any end

other than Armageddon, which they speak of
as if it were inevitable, even desirable, and never in doubt.

PRACTICING TO BE BOMBED ▲▼▲

1. Bushmaster

> *"In countries like the United States it's perfectly legal for*
> *members of the public to own certain types of firearms.*
> *If you live in such a country obtain an assault rifle legally,*
> *preferably an AK-47 or variations."*
> — Al Qaeda training manual

Back in Chicago I had a friend
we all thought was crazy,
largely because he insisted
there was no meaningless pun.

"They all mean something,"
he said, and Oscar Wilde
remarked that only the foolish
do not judge by appearances.

Is there an obvious pun, then,
in the fact that "Bushmaster"
is the name of the rifle used
by the D. C. snipers

and that the owner of Bushmaster
Firearms was chief fundraiser
in George W. Bush's campaign?
Fact: our President is against

all efforts at gun control, even
the modest proposals approved
by his idol and role model,
Ronald Reagan. But who

besides me and my friend Bernie,
last seen in Jimmy's Woodlawn
Tavern in Chicago, would make

anything of such accidental puns?

I know it's absurd even to notice.

11. Be Prepared !

The President who campaigned
as a uniter not a divider

is now head of the house most
divided in history,

and it was Abraham Lincoln,
to whom he compared himself,

who said that a house divided
against itself cannot stand.

It is only the blind and naïve
who no longer think the war

can come to our shores,
and not only in one spasmodic

attack like that of 9/11.
And therefore we should discuss

our options as we await the attacks.
You tell me you already take notice

of ditches you could leap into
and that fleeing hurricanes is good

practice for global warming as well.

III. The Decision

Have you decided, my dear,
where you wish to be
bombed? At home or out

in the rain? With me or
our dog at your side?
With Mozart on the phono

or maybe Ella Fitzgerald
singing scat that distracts?
If you want me to be present

as you did when you had
your trigger finger stitched
I could provide comfort,

assure you that it is not
likely to hurt — modern
weapons being what

they are. Perhaps, like
peasants, we too could be
caught in flagrante —

I would like that. Yet
I want you to be aware
of all options. Perhaps

you just prefer having tea
while we wait. Or we
might throw a party.

Or just sit in meditation —
certain that humming AUM
would give God our last word,

at least having that choice.

PARA LEVITAR EL PENTÁGONO ᴧᵧᴧ

— *Para Solomon Stucky, activista Quaker*

CLEPTOCRACIA: un gobierno dedicado a la avaricia desenfrenada, al robo y la corrupción, al saqueo a una gran escala internacional.

El Estanque Reflectante todavía sirve a Narciso.
El caballo de bronce en el Puente de Arlington
todavía se llama Valor, como se llamaba cuando Vietnam
era el país que bombardeábamos. La violencia superior
todavía se considera la más virtuosa
y todo lo que es bueno se logra por la espada.

Una guerra se ha cambiado por otra
de la misma ralea y diseño, Vietnam
e Irak, ambas erupciones de la misma infección.
Las guerras avanzan como las enfermedades y
el virus corona parece una corona
y ¿quién puede dudar que nuestro presidente lleva una,
pues es mimado y consentido
como cualquier reyezuelo de la historia? ¿Y qué clase de
rey? Cleptócrata, pues la suya es una guerra
para el robo, cleptomanía a gran escala,
para arrebatar el petróleo como los españoles arrebataron el oro.
Y ay del que se les atraviese.

En la década de los sesenta un grupo roquero
y cientos de manifestantes de toda la
nación canturreaban con la esperanza de
levitar el Pentágono, hacerlo levantarse
y desaparecer como un platillo volador,
acabar con toda la maldad que de ahí surgía,
un verdadero exorcismo.
Y mientras ellos salmodiaban
los coches fúnebres y los armones arrastrados por caballos
llevaban los cadáveres por el puente

LEVITATING THE PENTAGON ᴧ ɤᴧ

— for Solomon Stucky, Quaker activist

KLEPTOCRACY: A government devoted to rampant
greed, theft, and corruption, shoplifting on a grand
and international scale.

The Reflecting Pool still serves for Narcissus.
The bronze horse at the Arlington Bridge
is still named Valor as it was when Vietnam
was the land we were bombing. The superior
violence is still considered the more virtuous
and all that is good is brought by the sword.

One war has been exchanged for another
of the same breed and design, Vietnam
and Iraq both outbreaks of the same infection.
Wars proceed like disease, and the corona
virus has the look of a crown, and who
can doubt that our president wears one,
for he is as pampered and indulged
as any king in history. And what kind
of king? Kleptocratic, for his is a war
for theft, kleptomania on a grand scale,
out to grab oil as the Spaniards grabbed gold.
And woe to anyone who gets in the way.

Back in the Sixties a rock group
and hundreds of protesters from all over
the nation chanted in hopes they could
levitate the Pentagon, make it rise
and spin away like a flying saucer,
end all the evil emerging, a true exorcism.
And all the time they were chanting
the hearses and horse-drawn caissons
kept hauling the bodies across the bridge

al Cementerio de Arlington para que yacieran
con los muertos de todas las otras guerras
que se elogiaban en esa época.

Pero el Pentágono no salió volando
a las estrellas y la guerra continuó durante varios
años hasta que llegó el momento de enterrarla
y ocuparse de preparar la siguiente
con todo el genio del hombre para hacer y vender la matanza.

—Translated by Lilvia Soto

and into Arlington Cemetery to lie
with the dead of all the other wars
that were praised in their times.

But the Pentagon did not spin off into
the stars and the war went on for a few
more years until it was time to bury that one
and get very busy preparing for the next
with all man's genius to make and market the killing.

LOOKING BACK ⋏⋎⋏

The war plans were no secret,
you could read them in the papers,

follow arrows where the planes
and tanks would soon advance,

but we saw no children looking up,
seeking missiles far too fast to see.

The weapons were even smarter,
we were told, than those of Desert

Storm, since the years between
had not been wasted. Night

and day designers had worked away.
We now have oil as spoils of war

and on freeways watch it turn to smog.

VOWS OF SILENCE ESSENTIAL ⋏⋎⋏

At a magic stroke I'll stop —
my howling fellows foaming at the mouth —
and try to smile, if I still know how.
                    — Attila Jozsef, trans. by John Batki

There is no way to discuss the mess
that is this war. When I say over breakfast
that I am sick of the propaganda
that invades every news article — at least
one reminder per column of the crimes
of the sadist Saddam — my beloved tells me
that of course there should be lots of reminders
and that I "must not gloss over the crimes."
No, my love, I should not — and do not —
though I also refuse to gloss over those
of George Bush and his gang.

But one thing is clear. One should not —
even if with one's beloved — especially
with one's beloved — discuss a subject
as ugly as this war and its ongoing chaos
as one crime leads to another and the blame
is passed around like a hot potato.

This war is so ugly and divisive
we will soon blame each other
as the poison gas of it spreads
and brains full of toxins return home
to commit their inevitable crimes,
for many clones of McVey are in training.

With a vow to discuss war no more lest
along with clay gods bombed to oblivion
our lovely day will be blasted to hell, I retreat
to my cave of exile where in shadows
I honor words as if they could never do harm.

Fear of losing the only love left makes the task
Easy — not to volunteer for war even with words.
So let me wipe war from my mind in order
to honor a morning which might have inspired
Basho with a new haiku. Let me salute only
chrysanthemums and return alive to my love.

WMDs ANEW

On the freight siding
the cars of DuPont and Dow
stand ready to serve.

THE ETERNAL RETURN
TO THE SHADOWS ᴧᵥᴧ

"In a dark corner of the room
cries a helpless, crouching child..."
— Attila Jozsef, trans. by John Batki

How did I manage to crawl out and move around,
reach the small town and then move on to a city,

then another and another? Was I a ghost even then,
a wandering spirit ever tied to those shadows,

crawling into one new year, then looking back on it
from another? No one tried harder than I to make peace

and claim a place in the world, but again and again
I was turned back by a snarling face and a fist.

Back to the farm, back to the shack, back
to the cave of shadows — anything to make them happy.

Who am I to deny that they — the scorners and rejecters
and worshippers of mediocrity — own the world?

They no longer need to prove it to me. I open a magazine
and encounter a laundry list called poetry. I flick on

a television set and see the face of a puppet exalted.

ALIEN CITIES

"Only alien cities lie ahead."
— Mikhail Matusovsky

One by one they must be attacked,
for they have come within range
of our leader's righteous eyes.

His list is long, enough for
a few decades at least. A hundred
years war is not outside the range

of possibility. A humble man,
he admits that he along with the rest
of us will be dead by the time

ghosts of historians render their judgments.
Meanwhile he and his cohorts
assure us that all is for the best,

and reporters are still eager to agree.

RELIABLE PREDICTABILITY ▵▿▵

"The destructive man is reliability itself,"
wrote Walter Benjamin who,
as the Nazis took over, decided he should
either carry out his suicide plan or work
on his charming memoir of childhood.

How do we make sense of extremes,
he asked, in pursuing our "sparks
of holiness," living in the *Jetzt Zeit,*
the now time, when we must be cunning
if we are to survive and behold
the best of what each day offers,
although we are under no obligation
to accept even the miraculous gifts.

Whatever Der Führer did it would advance
the cause of death and deceit, leave the earth
ravaged, rich in corpses, rubble and ash.
As "destructive man" he was "reliability itself."

And one thing we know about our war-
loving leaders is that they too are reliable.
Whatever they say, whatever they do
is wholly reliable and ever a source
of unwelcome surprise and new deceit.
And whatever philosophers might make of it
there will be no need for their insights,
says our President, for "we'll all be dead."

WAR TOYS AT HOME
& ABROAD ▲▼▲

"One girl cut up into pieces
and eaten by soldiers" —
only a news report
which goes on to discuss
recruitment of children
as warriors — Uzis
handed out to them like toys.
But that is in Africa, no need
to intervene, and here at home
although more billions
are allocated to stop terrorists,
assault weapons once again
are as available as alcopop —
sweet booze to lure children.
A terrorist, of course,
must have cash if he buys.

As for recruitment for war,
roving pairs of marines
roam malls and ghettos,
reservations and taverns,
enticing with every promise
known to hook kids like fish.
No other options are mentioned
in brochures they are obliged
to read, although like the C.O.
Olaf in a poem by e.e. cummings
they could each assert that
"there is some s. I will not eat."
In a gentler voice the same poet
reminded us that
"there's a hell of a good universe next door."

PRE-EMPTIVE WAR ⚔

Do you have a problem explaining the terms
to a child, even to one bright enough
to ask if what you mean is just a "sneak attack"?

But most kids won't have heard of Pearl Harbor,
or give you a hard time by popping unwelcome
questions or making embarrassing comparisons.

They already know about smart bombs,
worshipped for years. Collateral damage
and unintended consequences are no-brainers

unless you are talking to kids with imaginations,
in which case they might envision themselves
blown apart. For that you'd need tranquilizers.

Ah, it helps so much in these Bushian times
to have no curiosity and to be of small brain.
Who wants a kid trembling with fear, knowing

too much? By good fortune the media
give us lots of practice living with schizophrenia.
In the same magazine we get the President's view

that his war "is bringing freedom to a benighted
land ... doing something very noble" and photographs
of the dead and dying lying in streets littered

with sandals of those who leapt out of them.
No need to worry. By the time your children
reach school age they should be totally numbed

and prepared to live in a world turned upside down.

PEINES SANGRIENTOS ⋏⋎⋏

Hemos observado a los creyentes azotarse
con látigo hasta que les sangra la espalda,
pero sólo recientemente hemos oído de mujeres
que se peinan hasta que les sangra el cuero cabelludo.

Cuando sienten que se acerca una gran tormenta
los animales se voltean contra el viento si no encuentran refugio.
Y cuando Troya quedó en ruinas y las guerras de venganza
parecían inevitables los muros fueron bastante altos

para arrojar de ellos a las criaturas destinadas a ser guerreros.

—Translated by Lilvia Soto

BLOODY COMBS ⋏⋎⋏

We have observed men of faith flail themselves
over their shoulders with whips until their backs
are bloody, but only of late have we heard of women
combing their own hair until their scalps bleed.

When they sense a great storm is on the way
animals turn against the wind if there is no shelter.
And when Troy was in ruins and wars of revenge
seemed inevitable the walls were useful heights

from which to hurl infants destined to be warriors.

A BIRD–LOVER LAMENTS
THE KILLING ▲▼▲

"Who sees with equal eye, as God of all,
A hero perish, or a sparrow fall..."
— Alexander Pope

New Year's Day and the President
is out shooting quail
on his 16,000 acre ranch.

You'd think he'd have had enough
of killing, but not at all,
for our President must kill quail,

their losses "militarily insignificant,"
as his generals say of the war
in which counting's a tedious chore.

The son has already surpassed
his father, for his war has so many
more casualties that sometimes

they are understated by hundreds.
A gold star mother clutching
a two-decades old teddy bear

demands to know if her child
is among the five hundred counted,
or overlooked among the others.

ONE OF THE PRIVILEGES

How fortunate for the makers of war
that the final insight as a man falls,
bleeds his life out on the sand,

cannot be recovered or shared,
nor can the lost soldier march back
to his commander and tell him

what he now knows, in whatever
way he might choose. Lucky indeed
are the makers of war, for they do not,

at least in this life, have to face the dead.

THE PEACEMAKERS ◣◥◣

All but a few gave their vote for the bombing.
All but a few became enthusiastic.
Between patriotic songs on the radio

we hear more urgings to deal
with the demons — and no one
suggests that we too are demons,

that we could be our own axis of evil.
Yet now and then I examine myself
in a mirror, searching for the smirk

of a war-loving citizen sure of his cause.

THE GOAL

Allen Ginsberg told us what we writers
and artists should be doing — "Trying
to disturb the balance of consciousness
in this lonely century/ Everyone sick ..."

Perhaps that was always the case.
Consider Brueghel, who lived in a time
when corpses were piled high and every
Protestant in the Netherlands was at risk
of execution. Charles V and Philip II
were the Hitlers of their day and in
other times, other places, the same story
played itself out to its bloody conclusion.

Just imagine, Allen, your struggle against
the Military Industrial Establishment
is already lost history, breath expended
in another century, stuffed fat with corpses.
We looked forward to a clean millennium,
free of murder. But imagine our naïveté!

Yet I praise our futile efforts, our going down
with our words the way soldiers fall in battles.

UNA OBRA MAESTRA DE MOLIÈRE ⋏⋎⋏

"A George W. Bush se le impuso la grandeza."
— Comentarista de la National Public Radio

Puedo imaginarme una obra que sólo Molière
podría escribir —

una comedia tan encantadora como "El médico
a palos."

Se llamaría "El Presidente
a palos."

Trataría de un protagonista que sube
al poder gracias a un fallo

de la maquinaria electoral. Sube a las tablas
como un pequeño Coloso,

pavoneándose, su andar como el de Napoleón.
No, pensándolo bien, su paso

es de simio, con los brazos que se columpian
arqueados a su lado.

Lee muy poco, piensa aún menos,
toma decisiones,

se jacta, con las tripas. Crea un paraíso
fiscal para los ricos,

elimina todos los controles de la contaminación del aire,
el agua y la tierra, los tratados

que prometen diferir Armagedón.
Y luego insiste

MOLIÈRE'S MASTERPIECE ▲▼▲

"George W. Bush had greatness thrust upon him."
— National Public Radio commentator

I can imagine a play that only Molière
could do justice to —

a comedy as enchanting as "The Doctor
In Spite of Himself."

It would be called "The President
In Spite of Himself."

It would feature a protagonist elected
to office by some malfunction

of machinery. He strides onto stage
like a little Colossus,

swaggering, his walk like Napoleon's.
No, on second thought, his

is a simian walk, with bowed arms
swinging at his sides.

He reads very little, thinks even less,
makes decisions,

he boasts, from the gut. He cancels
taxes due from the rich,

all controls on pollution of air, land,
and water, treaties

that promise to stave off Armageddon.
And then he insists

en una guerra como la de su padre, la que podría
llevarlo a la Grandeza

a Palos. Pero como dije,
sólo Molière —

o Shakespeare — estarían a la altura del argumento,
aquél para escribir

la comedia, la única versión que podríamos
tolerar, y éste

para representar sus horrores.

—Translated by Lilvia Soto

on a war like his father's, which could
lead to Greatness

In Spite of Himself. But as I say,
it would take Molière —

or Shakespeare — to do justice to the plot,
the former to write

the comedy, the only version we could bear
to watch, and the latter

to render its horrors.

ARMAGEDDON ▲▽▲

"The Christian Civilization of the West is responsible for the menace that hangs over it."
— Antoine de Saint-Exupéry

Asked how history will view
his "war against terror" President Bush

said there's no way to know,
since "we'll all be dead."

Knowing of his belief in Armageddon
as an inevitable conclusion

to human wisdom and folly, some
who heard that remark were anxious.

After all, it there's anyone with the power
to bring on Armageddon, it's a President.

And he's already said, "Bring 'em on!"
as if this war is all about football.

CIPRO TO THE RESCUE ▲▼▲

"Can one find another market like this?"
—— Rumi

Biological warfare may be "well within
the bounds of accepted practice,"

as our National Security Adviser puts it
of sudden missile attacks halfway

around the world, reducing a car full
of presumed enemies to scorched sand.

But selective, we hope, must be the attack ——
be it on us or on them —— for only the rich

can afford the cure unless the poor journey
to India where the capsules would not

bear the imprint of a corporation
that grew out of slave labor and the Nazi

economy.   Above all we must not break
the Law, must stay "well within the bounds

of accepted practice." A patent conferred
by God must be respected and therefore

many will bow down before it, be offered
as sacrifice.   And in the next election

the President who reminds us of these rules
                will run as a man of the people.

DÉJÀ VU ⋏⋎⋏

This leader is a very special head of state.
He can detain anyone he wants,
need give no explanation or say
where these people have disappeared to
or whether they will ever be released
or whether they are still alive.

His name, you might say, was Joseph Stalin.
His name, you might say, was Saddam Hussein.
But you would be living in the past,
back when *habeas corpus* did not mean
you may recover the corpse when we're done with it.

PORTRAITS OF GEORGE ▲▼▲

Here is the photo of his face in close-up,
the presidents of Mt. Rushmore behind him.

The suggestion is clear — that he belongs
among them — and multiple profiles will go

well on coins and stamps — worth the collecting —
a stimulation to the economy. And then too

we have George in his flight suit with every item
needed for emergencies dangling as if he might

need gas mask or pistol or knife at any moment
although the aircraft carrier is barely offshore.

But I also adore the portrait of George just sitting
as if thoughtful, with books shelved behind him,

although he is known to prefer news passed on
by his staff, the best source, these short briefings.

There are also portraits from Thanksgiving.
On the White House lawn he pardons a turkey,

a reprieve he does not extend to the troops in Iraq
as he leaves for dinner with them in Baghdad.

Returning, as Air Force One pours exhaust into ozone,
George spreads his palm on the shaved heads

of his Special Forces, the ones who rated a ride
home. They gaze upon him in adoration as if

he is saying: "Suffer the burly he-men to come
unto me!" High in the sky with gas guzzling

from all engines these men look like green angels
joking with God. With Baghdad far below

their commander is out of range for smelling
vaporized bodies or hearing gunfire from rubble,

a scene that not God but George hath wrought —
all, perhaps, for the portraits.

HITLER, BUSH
AND OTHERS ▲▼▲

*Liars hold nations
in thrall, lie ad absurdum.
Numbed world wakes too late.*

PYRAMIDS ⋏⋎⋏

Every world-class tyrant
should have himself

a pyramid of skulls
if he is to be worthy

of the tradition that includes
Genghis Khan and quite

a long list of successors,
Hitler, Stalin, and Saddam

among them. And after
he has enough skulls

for his pyramid he should
stop the collecting.

But knowing when to stop
requires wisdom rarely

found in those addicted to war.
And not even the U.N. demands it.

A UN NIÑO DE BAGDAD

"bombas inteligentes"
Eufemismo oficial

Nuestras bombas pueden todavía mandarte
a una vida mejor. Tú y tu loro erótico
pueden aún intercambiar sus posiciones. Te damos,
por lo menos, una oportunidad de mejorarte.

Tal vez puedas nacer bajo
una estrella afortunada la próxima vez, quizás vivir
en nuestra tierra de leche y miel
y bombardear tú también.

Dicen que morirás este año,
que nuestras bombas lo hicieron — los apagones,
las aguas contaminadas, ese tipo de cosa —
pero exageran.

Si conocieras estas bombas te encantarían.
Les dibujamos caras sonrientes. Les sacamos
brillo y les ponemos nombres de mascotas.
Mandamos a prisión a los que las insultan.

Y son *inteligentes* — así fué como te encontraron.

— Translated by Lilvia Soto

TO A CHILD OF BAGHDAD ▲▼▲

"smart bombs"
Official euphemism

Our bombs may yet blast you
to a better life. You and your vivid parrot
may even change places. We give you
a chance, at least, to better yourself.

Who knows, you may be born beneath
a lucky star next time, maybe live
in our land of milk and honey,
and do some bombing yourself.

They say you'll die this year,
that our bombs did it — the power outage,
polluted water, that sort of thing —
but they'd be stretching a point.

If you knew these bombs you would love them.
We draw smiley faces on them. We keep them
spit-shined and give them pet names.
We throw people in prison for insulting them.

And they are *smart* — that's how they found you.

INNOVACIONES ▲▼▲

Éste es un nuevo sesgo — "la guerra preventiva,"
más gloriosa que las anteriores,

la emprendieron sólo para defender una patria.
No existe nada semejante en la historia —

esta idea novedosa — como Pearl Harbor
o las Cruzadas.

—Translated by Lilvia Soto

INNOVATIONS ▲▼▲

This is a new twist — "preemptive war,"
more glorious than the old kind,

undertaken only to defend a homeland.
There is nothing like it in history —

this novel idea — like Pearl Harbor,
or the Crusades.

A CAPTIVITY NARRATIVE

All reports regarding the rescued soldier
describe her as "young" and "beautiful,"

only nineteen — the perfect age for the tale —
another captivity narrative, as when

a kidnapped white maiden was taken
to live in a teepee. But by good fortune

Private Lynch was rescued — a magnificent
story — welcome for the uses of propaganda.

And who would not wish her well?
Yet it was an Iraqi doctor who risked

his life and trudged across the desert
to summon her rescuers, and the story

need not be told in a way that suggests
the enemy's villainy, as were the Indian

captivity narratives, which served hate
and fear. It was not only our own

Special Forces who rescued this woman,
though in the reenactment that was the case.

But when it comes to myth making
the truth must not stand in the way

even when the heroine objects.
We like to stick to the classic formulas

such as Noh drama and Western movies,
as when our President puts on his cowboy boots

and his Stetson and waves his guns all around.

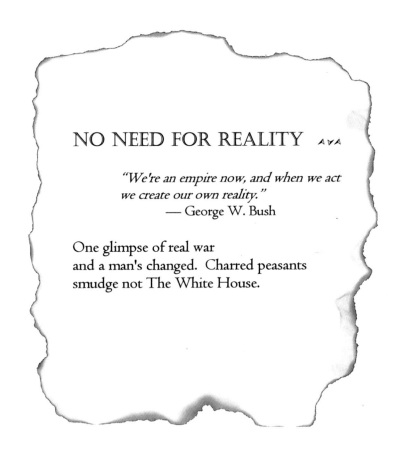

NO NEED FOR REALITY ⋀ⵗ⋀

*"We're an empire now, and when we act
we create our own reality."*
— George W. Bush

One glimpse of real war
and a man's changed. Charred peasants
smudge not The White House.

BITTER OLEANDERS △▽△

Our yard has such a tall stand
of poison beauties that they block

our view to the west, but it never
occurred to me to take a bite of a leaf

or a blossom, although I have often
risked my life on a foolish impulse.

Just think of it — so much potential
for death right here in our yard!

Warplanes at practice roar overhead
and we're supposed to be grateful

they do not drop their bombs on us
but just weave a gray flannel sky

and rattle our windows, crack
our plaster. Even oleanders

take their share of the sifting
particulates, the bitter rain,

the carcinogenic wake of war
dispersed until some people say

they can't smell it. Such denial,
it is claimed, is the mark of patriots —

as if they volunteer to eat oleanders,
        and declare they are sweet.

DOUBLETHINK & NEWSPEAK
ALIVE AND WELL ᴧᵛᴧ

There seems to be a confusion about the word
"politics," whether it's just a dog fight or a struggle
of humans to stay alive, and for some to speak truth.

For example, The New York Times, which in May
"reviewed shortcomings in its own reporting
about the events leading up to the war in Iraq"

(meaning that they helped establish the entrenched
lies that are still being told) denied permission
to reprint the article because "we are determined

not to associate ourselves with any work in film
or print that attacks either candidate. Our note,
'The Times and Iraq' was not intended to become

part of a political battle." In other words their
earlier propaganda which in May was declared
inoperative is now restored without amendment.

George Orwell would appreciate this apolitical
decision by editors who in the 2000 election seemed
to do all they could to get George Bush elected.

Has the truth yet been compared with Play-Doh,
or would I be the first poet to use such a simile,
although it might offend friends of the first family?

THE PRESCIENCE
OF GARCIA LORCA ◢▾◣

Surely a war is not simply a poem gone wrong
or proved right, yet Lorca tells us in poems
that when we take a wrong road we wind up

in blinding snow. We follow leaders blindfolded
by theories, men who know little of history
and have no humility. They topple statues,

then climb on the vacated plinths. And because
of the wrong turn and the blindfolded leaders
who have told us to lift to our lips the chalice of death

we wind up with a harvest of corpses so heavy the earth
would sink under them if we did not cart them away.
Lorca wrote that when we follow the blind we sentence

posterity to starvation or to graze weeds in cemeteries.

AFTER GARCIA LORCA ▲▼▲

"Mi amor humano!"
— Garcia Lorca

When you wake before the other
and feel you are standing guard
although you have no weapon

and your house seems made of straw
is it not a good time to give thanks?
Consider the red rose waiting for dawn

though its petals tremble from warplanes.

Yet Another War:

A SEQUENCE FOR
WILLIAM STAFFORD

Photograph of WILLIAM STAFFORD by GAIL GREGG

Friends

Bill Stafford called the world Friend,
and that's the right attitude, for sure.

But does it require intelligence
or a lapse in awareness? Is such

a commendable perspective naïve,
foolish, ingenuous, or even insincere?

Aren't we always doubtful or suspicious
of people who regard the world as a Friend?

Aren't there a few things they seem
to have forgotten? Or did Bill simply have

a subtle sense of humor when he spoke to
and of the world in a certain whimsical

way as a Friend, forgetful of massacres?
I, as Bill's Friend and the World's,

give him the benefit of the doubt,
but it takes some doing on a day when

the front page is devoted to full-color,
a father holding his bleeding son in his arms

as he cries to the sky, Why? Why?
in a language no one bothers to translate.

Music As Medicine

"What heals/ the city, its citizens, I know nothing about."
— Maxine Kumin

What music the names of cities once were,
and music poured out through their streets
and the dancers flung themselves ecstatic
into the night and children sang loud with joy.

Baghdad and Basra, Fallujah and Najaf, Baquba,
Khaldiya, Kirkuk and Iskandariya.
There was magic in names and great healing
to be found in music and the magic of names.

But do not tell me that the roar of jet planes
and tanks and bursting of missiles and rattle
of machine guns is even the most dissonant

music. Only when we again hear songs
in the streets can we seek out a cure
for our sorrow in Baghdad, Fallujah, or Kirkuk.

Unwelcome Visions

"It is time for all the heroes to go home."
— William Stafford

He had a vision as he walked the mall
where the corridors seemed a mile long.
In the swarm of people
he saw not one familiar face,
but he thought he saw sheep
shoving and edging past one another,
heads over shoulders, nudging
ear to ear, cushioned by wool,
their faces frozen with prim mouths.
He thought he heard them baaing,
nodding fiercely at products in windows.
And he looked around for the dogs
sure to be at work herding, nipping
at heels. Never had he been so hungry
for breeze from the sea and a green headland.
In the parking lot he had to stop himself
from diving under a van when planes
overhead swooped low in practice.
He saw that missiles were mounted under wings
and the sky was again trembling with war.

A Vision Emergency

As he saw night shroud his town
the poet wondered if we could ever

rescue the light, recover the good
we always relied on — the happenings

of everyday life. Peasants are fleeing
our planes, and we who fund a war

machine, even the gentlest among us,
are no longer the good people even

in our own eyes. Fear gathers around
towns and cities all over the earth

and we are what is feared, as Rome
once was, and our hills and walls

are not high enough to save us from those
we provoke or from barbarians within,

whom we have chosen as our masters.

For William Stafford, Conscientious Objector

We've got another war this year,
and under this barter system

it may well come down to a barrel
of blood for each one of oil

to be shipped back for our engines.
When they sent you to a work camp

in the mountains a man who was there
for murder could not figure it out —

how you were treated just like him
because you would not do what he did.

Strange world, he decided. And you
yourself were amazed daily

as the breezes through pines
confirmed your conviction

that to say no was the only true way
to say yes.

The Poet Almost Always Regrets Reading the Paper and if the President Does Not, Why Should the Poet?

"Fools . . . you have just helped elect that man!"
—William Stafford

Yet another story in the morning paper,
and you'd have read it over breakfast
after you'd have produced a new poem or two.

You'd have read of the war praised
as a great undertaking, and new heroes-to-be
profiled. The editors — as you know from other wars —

are willing propagandists. No one makes them
go along with the lies, and add a few of their own.
I can imagine your cynic eyes, how you would

look down upon that newspaper spread upon the table.
An observer might mistake your downcast eyes
for scorn, but then see the sorrow of one who loved peace.

Variations on a Line by William Stafford

"The darkness around us is deep."
—William Stafford

The darkness around us is deep,
cheap, or not. Coined in all sizes.
It seems there is no one unwilling
to give a gratuity — fund more

darkness, get it heaped on our plates —
more of the stuff we once swore
to evade, leave forever behind us.
It is easy indeed to request

the Dark Bitter, savor the taste,
join the dark, let shadows caress
us. Easy indeed it is to go to war,
come late to the truth. Shadows

join shadows, ever deeper. Stafford
made it sound simple, as if it's no
problem to bear the dark burdens.
He could say without even a wince:

"There is always more darkness . . ."

The Darkness Ever Deeper

Once I traveled through the dark with a friend
I knew was enlightened, as wise a man
as I have ever known, and I felt a great chill,
an immense distance between us as he drove.
As I chattered away, still unprofitable
to myself, he gazed at the road, headlights
clearing away darkness as he drove calmly
through the night. And in that dim light
within the car I suffered the envy of one
who knows he is lost, knows that the man
beside him is not. I felt it burn in my gut,
as if the liquor had put it there. He, of course,
never touched the stuff, and he arose
every morning at dawn to practice his art
and his devotions. How could that be forgiven?

I hungered for the enlightenment he seemed
to deny me, forsaking his duty to share.
And yet the contempt I felt for his liquorless
life was destroying me. I knew just one thing:
enlightenment could have led us out of that forest
in record time. It need not take years if he would
just tell me his secret. But my friend drove on,
right on the limit, and braked for a leaping deer.
Damn him, I thought — his wisdom lost us that deer.

DAVID with DOROTHY and WILLIAM STAFFORD / photo by JUDY RAY.

HOW FAR NEXT TIME ▴▾▴

How far next time? The first fellow
who picks up a long stone
and invents the hammer
sounds impressive, but a lobster
on the seafloor can do that.

And a log rolling along
will be a no-brainer since
every child will know the wheel
has just been invented. Then comes
what and in what order?

All that can be predicted is that
once again homo sapiens
will start with the stone and the wheel.
Computers melted upon the sands
will be of no use to figure out
where to go next. But start
with the stone, move on to the wheel.

The airplanes will reappear
like lungfish out of the sea
but this time they will not
bear bombs and darken the earth.
For someone, seeking the first virtue,
will know when or where to stop.

A MAN WITHOUT A COUNTRY

— for Mahmoud Darwish

As he sat before an official
Mahmoud was asked to prove
that he existed as he sat there

requesting a passport since
as a child in his father's arms
he had fled the nation at war,

thus giving up his right
to citizenship in the land
of his birth. Before he had

access to words such as those
he now used in poems
he had denied himself rights

both to travel or obtain
a residency card for return
to his birthplace. He pleaded

that he did in fact exist
since he was sitting there,
but began to doubt it himself.

(Had he not read Kafka
he might not have believed
what was taking place.)

Please then, he said, may I
have permission to go jump
into the sea? I am sorry,

replied the officer. That sea
is now part of our nation

and you are not. Therefore

I do not have the authority
to grant you a permit.
Darwish looked to the sky.

THE MAN WHO NEVER MADE A MISTAKE ◣◥◣

The president was perplexed
when a reporter asked, "What
has been your biggest mistake?"

He took several minutes trying
to think of one, but could not.
Obviously it was a sincere effort.

Or perhaps he was being subtle,
just making the dead air space
available for us to think of a few.

REINVENTING HELL ▲▼▲

"And men were delighted that once more they
were led like sheep."
— Dostoyevsky

How they long to be enslaved,
to have a dictator they can adore.
How willing they are to disregard
their own interests, become cogs
in the machine (off to war if told to)
or mere flesh no more important
than what is pounded into lunch meat
or ground up as burgers.

How they long for a Savior,
"God's messenger," and how willing,
even eager, they are to take
his word for it that he is the Second
Coming (glad to be spared, however,
the crucifixion of the First). Oh,
he has long been awaited!
Let us sing Hallelujah in joyful song.

According to our new Savior
Armageddon is desirable and he
will do his best to make sure
it arrives on time just as St. John
predicted. But another school
of thought is that God meant for us

to ignore foolish and paranoid prophecies.

PETITION ◣▾◢

*"Chichén Itzá contains temple pyramids, the largest
known ballcourt in Meso-America, and a tzompantli
(skull platform). From the Great Plaza a causeway
leads to the Cenote (Well) of Sacrifice, a massive
pit into which votive offerings and human sacrifices
were cast."*
— The Cambridge Encyclopedia

Please take our sons, our daughters too,
those who wish to save for college

with the modest pay of a soldier,
those who cannot find work in town

or on the reservation — nothing better than
minimum wage, and nothing with benefits

or even false promises. Come and get them,
invite them to your war. Allure them

with posters and commercials.
And threaten them with fines if they fail

to register for the draft that is forthcoming.
Yet a better tactic might be to convince them

that to be chosen as prince or princess
and thrown into the pit called a cenote is an honor.

QUAGMIRES ▲▼▲

— After Thich Nhat Hanh

A mosque this time, and not one pagoda.
A village of clay rather than bamboo or straw.
Sand aswirl everywhere, stirred by the rotors
of helicopters and winds that sting faces.

There are no rivers exploding, flinging mud
and dead fish. The same stars burn on
overhead. Others on earth are alive
and oblivious. Those who denounce war

are disregarded. Those who order the killing
are far away from the blood striking sand.
They lose no sleep. They take long vacations.
None of their children show up on casualty lists.

Gazing at a page of photographs, America's
dead of only one week, my mourning for them
comes in waves, for I lack the immunity
that protects those who approve this war.

THE TOUR ▲▼▲

An American's amazed on his visit
to Vietnam to look down into a web
of tunnels — a vast labyrinth that served
the Viet Cong for decades. No grenades

or gas could rout them, for always more
rushed through those corridors from North
to South to replace the blasted soldiers.
And the guide for the tour group explains

that the tunnel's bore was quite precise –
just right for Asian men and women,
but a trap for the well-fed foe. The guide
adds that tunnels will soon be enlarged,

since tourists wish to crawl those routes,
progress like moles within those holes —
for on any battlefield a visitor will long
to imagine all that happened yet manage

surviving intact where their lost fathers died.

COUNTERPOINT ᴀᵛᴀ

— After Thai Luan and Trung Sinh

"When you leave," the Viet Cong said,
"the bamboo will still be creaking in the wind
and lime trees will be growing new leaves
and jackfruit will ripen in gardens
and later the withered leaves of the lime trees
will be falling. Meanwhile, when one boy
is killed another boy is available."

And then he added, "Or perhaps the war
could have ended today. Or perhaps next year."

A HORN HEARD AROUND THE WORLD ᴀᵛᴀ

In the streets of an Iraqi town
halfway around the globe

an oogah-oogah horn of an old Model A
is brought to my ears by a radio

and I am back in Oklahoma —
those dusty streets, those lost faces,

those black rusty flivvers,
wobbling jalopies driven by ghosts.

PONTITO & OTHER TOWNS ⏶⏷⏶

*"The insurgents don't have the support of the people here,"
Colonel Bishop said. "They now know the local populace
is working with us against them."*
— *The New York Times*, May 8, 2004

There's an Italian who paints towns
with no people in them,
as if a neutron bomb did its work
back in the middle ages but left

all the charm of those towns intact.
I would love to take my wife there
and we could be the first in hundreds
of years to stroll those narrow streets,

wander into a trattorìa and warm up
some pasta left in the pan when the cook
and everyone else disappeared as if
ascended in the rapture or vaporized,

then we could take our pick of rooms
in the most charming of pensiones
along the harbor where quaint boats
rocking in moonlight would enchant us.

Was it that painter from Pontito who
inspired the word-artists who report
on the war, describe progress through
"the warrens and alleyways of cities"

empty of all residents other than rebels,
insurgents, and "militiamen prepared
to fight to the death"? The news photos
show our soldiers lobbing grenades over

walls higher than themselves. Other shots
show snipers firing fusillades into the
distance. Just like Pontito, it seems
the town is empty of civilians except

for one "man in a beige robe who writhed in
a pool of blood for half an hour before
falling still." He must have been the painter,
the only resident of the otherwise empty

town, an artist whose favorite color was red.

AUNTIE JOAN AND OTHERS ◢▼◣

Auntie Joan was a good woman
and we are grateful she made it
to ninety-three and a few days beyond.

We could still be sitting in her flat
in Sussex where she lived
with her photos of lost ones —

those who had died or grown up.
She served us tea and biscuits,
then we walked around the garden

shared with other pensioners.
Our memories of her are all good
and we mourn her because

of particular details. There was much
of Auntie Joan to keep in mind,
very vivid, even her handkerchief

and the fat china teapot she lifted
and the way she smiled even at me,
a stranger brought in from abroad.

But of those vaporized in Iraq
we know little and thus our grief
is generic and without tears

and we are left numbed and leaden.
We are told they were *collateral*

damage, unintended consequences.

Yet I need to weep for them.
Auntie Joan has given me tears enough
for at least a dozen, but I need more

for children who are ash in the rubble.

SIGNS

A week into the war
the President was exempted
from future prosecution
for war crimes.

Now what did that tell us
about how it would go?

AIRPORT SECURITY ᴀᴥᴀ

In the airport I got wanded,
though not by a fairy princess.

I had to remove my shoes,
prove they were not twin bombs.

But the strangest scene I saw
that day was where random checks

delayed the suspicious —
the grey lady in her wheelchair

and the toddler boy tugged
from his mother's hand, pulled

through the metal detector's arch.
She tried to follow but was

restrained by two guards who grasped
her arms as she yelled, "But I told

him not to talk to strangers!"
The child wailed bloody murder.

A female guard patted the boy
all over, although he did not giggle.

I myself went on profiling terrorists.
                 They were so obvious.

MISSILE SHIELD ⋀⋁⋀

We have been here before.
As Frenchmen we breathed easy
because we had that Maginot line.

As Americans we trusted
planes and battleships and our
manifest destiny to prevail, invincible.

We have been here so many times
we are dizzy, and yet
there are still those young enough,

green and untested enough, unwise
and unhumble enough to think
a high wall in the sky can keep out

killer bees. Fence off the sea,
electrify every shore, and the shark
will prevail, and somewhere, just

somewhere, there's a young man
clever enough to rent a truck
and deliver a bomb, or just buy

a Bushmaster rifle.

A PORTRAIT
OF ALBERT EINSTEIN ▲▼▲

It is only an old poster on the wall —
a black and white portrait of Einstein,
his right eye half closed, his left
cynical, penetrating, directed
at the viewer as if to demand something.
And what could that something be?
Would it by chance concern his conclusion
that his life's work had been perverted
by the makers of wars and bombs?

"Ach," he moaned on August 6, 1945,
when he heard the news from Hiroshima,
"This has changed everything except
the way man thinks." Later he added
that he would never have lifted a finger
had he known the Nazis would not
have got the bomb. Therefore I can guess
what he demands of us as he looks out
of the past with such intensity — no less
than changing the way we think.

The poster includes a bold caption:
GREAT SPIRITS HAVE ALWAYS
ENCOUNTERED VIOLENT OPPOSITION
FROM MEDIOCRE MINDS. Mice
with mediocre minds have nibbled
holes in Einstein's fluffy hair and brain.

Though I do not seek out irony
I often glance up and find it hard to avoid
          as I regard the challenging portrait.

"OPPENHEIMER CELEBRATION EXAMINES MYTH & MAN" △▽△
– NEW YORK TIMES

Choosing a site for his Manhattan
Project, J. Robert Oppenheimer

recalled the Eden of his youth,
then turned it into glowing nuclear

waste sites, six hundred at last count
around Los Alamos. The crowd

gathers to celebrate Oppie's hundredth
birthday, he who unleashed a beast

more fearsome than any in history.
Of course we still imagine that if we

are the masters of that beast, restrain it
like a trained bear, we will never suffer

the fate doled out to the Japanese.
On a train as Oppenheimer crossed

America on his way to the work,
he read through *The History of the*

Decline and Fall of the Roman Empire,
although he did not, perhaps, think

long and hard enough about the
Decline and Fall of our planet earth.

THE ATOMIC TRAIL ▲▼▲

"Parents, she said, could take their children along an
atomic trail."
— *New York Times*

What Ms. Kelly of The Atomic Heritage Foundation
means is that the great heroes of the Twentieth Century

include Oppenheimer and Teller, and that their Little
Boy and Fat Man were wondrous inventions.

She means the little children should be led as by a pied
piper through "a discontinuous national park

that would include missile silos in Montana; remnants
of weapons complexes at Hartford, Washington;

the Oak Ridge, Tennessee, National Laboratory;
and dozens of other historic places!" I can see

the children being led past these sacred sites,
peering down into the missile silos, gazing in awe

at the guide who praises the weapons, instills
a profound love of them. I have seen children

led through the Krispy Kreme bakery and given
logo hats and samples of seven kinds of do-nuts

as the pied piper speaks of the wonders, where
the home factory is and when it began turning out

do-nuts, and how many thousands are baked
every day at this site and that. Within an hour

a hundred kids are turned into addicts.
They'll be hooked on Krispy Kremes for life.

At Los Alamos where the atomic trail begins
new generations at risk of genetic mutations

can be led through the chambers of horrors
to which like children they are already addicted.

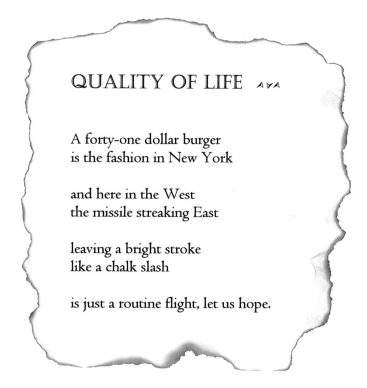

QUALITY OF LIFE

A forty-one dollar burger
is the fashion in New York

and here in the West
the missile streaking East

leaving a bright stroke
like a chalk slash

is just a routine flight, let us hope.

"TELL ME, PHIL,
CAN YOU SEE FALLOUT?" ▲▼▲

> *"Even a thousand bombs will not of themselves decide
> the issue of a major war. We said there is no defense,
> and we meant it."*
>
> — Philip Morrison

Strange grit had fallen
from the sky above our redwood
picnic table, and the children
pointed up, scared because
they had never seen such an eerie
yellow glow, a powdered mist.

My boy said he could feel it
on his hands, and rubbed it
like sand or mica. And the girl
climbed upon her mother's knee
and demanded to be hugged.
And yet, I thought, this is just
the light pointillists so loved,
as if it broke the world down
to tiny points which dance
before our fervid eyes. Imagine
that — the world dissolved
or exploded into fragments!

Naïve indeed to ask — a question
such as children pose. "Can
you see fallout?" But who
would know best if not my pal,
the nuclear physicist, for he
had stood on white sand
on the fated horrid day of Trinity.
As if to assembled children
he might take upon his knees
he replied, "Oh, it's there all right,

but not that obvious. Of course
it's everywhere." His words
were spoken in a tone that said
"Go in peace, my children, for none
escape the perils of their time.
It's the bombs themselves we fear,
and let the fallout go." And then
he laughed a bitter laugh and said:
"We feel like Dr. Frankenstein.
Our monster ran away, but no crowd
will ever chase that monster down."

DISSIDENT ▲▼▲

I too honor war,
for I would show up, stand stunned,
flagless at such parades.

LA MUERTE DE SARDANÁPALO △▽△

*También conocido como Asurbanipal, rey de Asiria antes
de la caída de Nínive en el siglo VII a. de J. C.*

Cansado de resistir el asedio,
Sardanápalo el asirio,
recostado sobre su lecho carmesí,
la cabeza sobre el brazo,
su corona de oro en la mano,
observaba con mirada indiferente
la masacre a su alrededor — preparada toda
como tributo a su grandeza.

Sus concubinas, desnudas excepto
por los aretes y brazaletes de oro
para brazos y tobillos,
fueron arrastradas ante él de todos lados,
los brazos inmovilizados
por los esclavos.
Parecen renuentes
en el cuadro de Delacroix
donde espadas y garrotes
aseguran una escena sangrienta
antes del incendio final que engolfa
a esclavos y espadachines.
El último sobreviviente arroja
la antorcha y asi los enemigos que
avanzan encuentran muy poco botín
como recompensa por sus esfuerzos.

En una cartelera de Bagdad,
Saddam Husayn, alto y orgulloso
en su carro de oro, se refirió
a sí mismo como la reencarnación
de reyes antiguos, pero en los textos
inscritos en barro no es fácil
saber cuál.

—Translated by Lilvia Soto

THE DEATH OF SARDANAPALUS ᴀᵥᴀ

*Also known as Ashurbanipal, who reigned as king
before the fall of Ninevah in the 7ᵗʰ Century B.C.*

Sardanapalus the Assyrian,
tired of holding out against a siege,
lay back upon his crimson bed
and with indifferent gaze,
head propped upon his arm,
palm cupping his crown of gold,
observed the massacre
around him — all prearranged
as tribute to his greatness.

His concubines, arms pinned
by slaves, were dragged
before him from all sides,
women naked except
for golden bracelets, anklets,
earrings. They look reluctant
in the painting by Delacroix
where swords and garroting
assure a bloody scene before
the final fire, which will engulf
each slave and swordsman.
The last man standing flings
the torch, and thus the enemies
advancing find little loot
for all their trouble.

Saddam Hussein on a Baghdad
billboard stood tall and proud
in a golden chariot and spoke
of himself as the reincarnation
of ancient kings, but in texts
inscribed in clay it is not
an easy task to say which one.

The Death of Sardanapalus by Eugene Delacroix [FRENCH, 1827;

INSPIRED BY THE PLAY "SARDANAPALUS" BY GEORGE GORDON, LORD BYRON.]

SURVIVORS ▲▼▲

"They are being manipulated by the warmakers."
—Allen Ginsberg

Not long after World War II an instructor
in a class at the University of Chicago
projected on the wall a slide of Guernica,
a painting by Picasso inspired by the dive
bombing of a village in Spain. But a girl
who had survived the war began screaming
and threw her arms up as if bombs were again
falling upon her. She could have modeled
for the painting, which shows the same reaction.

And several wars later, knowing the power
of that painting, General Colin Powell,
selling a new war to the U.N., had the picture
draped lest it show in the background.
Fielding polite questions from deferential
journalists, General Powell had no desire
to deal with the troubling images of Guernica.

For smooth running of a propaganda machine
not even a glimpse of the real thing is permitted.
In a similar instance of draping works of art
likely to be seen in the background John
Ashcroft, another member of the team, spent
eight thousand dollars of tax money to drape
a nude statue of Aphrodite, the goddess of love.
What is it, one wonders, that scares the hell
out of these warriors? Art? Women? Truth?
An unscripted question?

SOBREVIVIENTES ⋏⋎⋏

"Los manipulan los alcahuetes de la guerra."
-- Allen Ginsberg

Poco después de la Segunda Guerra Mundial un instructor
de la Universidad de Chicago
proyectó en la pared una diapositiva de Guernica,
el cuadro de Picasso inspirado en el bombardeo
del pueblo vasco del mismo nombre. Una chica
que sobrevivió la guerra empezó a dar alaridos
y elevó los brazos al cielo como si de nuevo
le calleran las bombas encima. Podía haber sido la modelo
del óleo que muestra la misma reacción.

Varios años más tarde, conociendo el poder
de esa pintura, el General Colin Powell,
que trataba de vender una nueva guerra a las Naciones Unidas, dió
órdenes de cubrir el cuadro para que no apareciera en su presentación.
Al contestar las preguntas corteses de los periodistas
deferentes, el General Powell no quiso
hacer frente a las imágenes inquietantes de Guernica.

Para que la maquinaria de la propaganda funcione
sin problema alguno
no se permite ni un solo vistazo a la realidad.
En un intento similar de ocultar una obra de arte
que podría de otra manera verse en el fondo John
Ashcroft, otro miembro del equipo, gastó
ocho mil dólares del patrimonio nacional para cubrir
una estatua desnuda de Afrodita, la diosa del amor.
¿Que será lo que tanto asusta a estos guerreros?
¿El arte? ¿Las mujeres? ¿La verdad?
¿Una pregunta inesperada que no aparece en el guión?

—Translated by Lilvia Soto

SPAIN ▴▾▴

I spoke today for a while
of the Spanish Civil War, which none of them
had heard of, being born far too late
and too indifferent. I spoke of Francisco Franco
and King Alfonso and Lorca who was shot
and Guernica the bombed fishing village, the dive
bombers, screaming Stukas, and the hands flung up
to the skies. I spoke of the red Spanish earth
used as testing ground for German planes and bombs
for the big war ahead, a murderous warm-up
while the Allies did nothing, though they let the Fascist guns
get through. I spoke of the Hegelian dialectic
crunching its way through its notches like an old ratchet
serving a rusty well in the rocky ground,
and I described the Spanish village where I lived for a Winter,
where some of the Loyalist men had not yet emerged
from hiding places in attics and cellars thirty years after the war.

Franco was still alive and in charge. I also got to know
the grocer who had had his rival shot so he could have
both stores, but I didn't bother them with information
like that or how they would say it had all been a long time ago,
though the bullet holes from the firing squads were still
in the whitewashed wall on the hill. And last I spoke
of how as a boy in a small Oklahoma town I often saw
the skinny man with an eyepatch and a crutch for one leg,
which he had left in Spain when he fought in the Lincoln Brigade.
I told how we boys would taunt him and make fun of his black beret
as he sat on the curb outside the Oasis Bar and Grill,
his crutch beside him, its rubber tip in the gutter. I mentioned
how he was condemned by every drunk inside as a Commie.
When we learned to play pool, that word came with the lesson.
And then I spoke of how I wish I had gone and sat beside him.

WARNING ᴬᵧᴬ

You will own this war,
General Powell warned the President,
speaking as if it could be dropped

and broken into so many shards
that not even two could be glued
back together. But then to the world

the General read the script
he was given, saying nothing
about what might be shattered.

ADVERTENCIA ᴬᵧᴬ

Usted será el dueño de esta guerra,
advirtió el General Powell al Presidente,
hablando como si fuera algo que pudiera dejarse caer

y quebrarse en tantos fragmentos
que ni siquiera dos pudieran volver
a pegarse nunca más. Pero entonces el General

le leyó al mundo el guión
que le dieron y no dijo nada
de lo que podía hacerse añicos.

—*Translated by Lilvia Soto*

MUSIC DRIVEN OUT
EVERY MOMENT WE LIVE ◢◥◢

*"Time is running out
and maybe the world was made
by your enemy in his image
not yours."*
— Paul Pines

I wake from a dream, am not sure
if I wish to re-enter it, learn
its wisdom. I betray and forsake

it for the radio news. Thus the war
drives out my dream, which
could not be half so horrid.

Have we waded so deep in blood,
gone so far into the dark
that we prefer it, wallow in war,

can't get enough of it, choose
propaganda over silence or music,
as if this war has become polyphonic

while poor Mozart and Bach
play their melodic hearts out, go
begging attention on other channels?

And how much shame must I bear
for being witness to this war,
guest at this orgy, heeding its plea

with bombast of bombs for total attention?

OUR FAIR-HAIRED BOY

The President, running for election
the weekend he allows the assault
weapons ban to expire, reminds us
that he holds every life precious,
although we don't hear much grief
coming from him or his cabal for
those he has sent to their deaths.

A foolish lover of truth may well protest,
listing a catalogue of woes — a crippled
economy, millions unemployed, corporate
thieves given license to steal, thousands
of Afghanis and Iraqis killed, cultural heritage
of two nations hammered and bombed
into oblivion, hundreds of Americans
sacrificed, denied their chance one day
to be President or at least to vote a few
times in their lives and maybe become
fathers and mothers. Needless to say,
destruction of habitat runs rampant. Few
birds are heard in the Garden of Eden
as the sun each day rises to new absurdities,
assaults on sanity, revelations of secret deals
while the worst of them are buried deep
as bodies bulldozed into mass graves.

But expose even a part of this and the people
who praise this man as if he is the new Messiah
will say, "But you've got to admit he is handsome
and charming, and a good family man
who believes in basic American values."
Those who know nothing of history
and how millions worshipped Hitler's forelock
need not think of other occasions, thus may agree.

THE COLOR SCHEME ʌʏʌ

It is left up to the polluters, how much
poison they choose to spew into the air.

And therefore we have pollution alerts,
though there's not much we breathers

can do to protect ourselves. Even over
the President's ranch it might be purple today,

which is what ground zero on 9/11 might
have been had a system been in place.

In Dallas and Houston it is best not
to venture outdoors at all. Prayer

for return of green or at least yellow
(which is not so bad) is advised.

Orange hurts those with sensitive lungs,
but all human lungs are somewhat sensitive.

Tangerine is predicted for tomorrow
and it is hoped that the great state of Texas

will be favored with thunderstorms.
For a minimal dose of ozone, get up

before sunrise. We could rename this air
Terrorist Air and be quite accurate,

for its surgical strikes are, alas, no more
precise than those delivered by bombers.

ALL MY SONS
AND A FEW DAUGHTERS ▲▼▲

"Inspired by what faith
am I to fight this war?"
— Kondo Yoshimi

My wife and I often have the pool to ourselves,
arrive while the klieg lights are still on along
with those underwater, although it is past dawn.

But this morning we came across an odd sight
and were ordered down to the children's end,
shallow water where paddling along we watched

what seemed a strange session of training. Two
or three dozen R.O.T.C. students in camouflage battle
suits were lined up in a queue and one by one shoved

into the water by an officer who yelled in each face.
Mind you, these young pretend soldiers were wearing
full battle dress of tropical green with leaves and dark

shadows. They were wearing black boots that came up
over their ankles. They held rifles before them with both
hands as if in supplication as they approached an officer,

then accepted his order to stand in the line and be shoved.
These young men and women wore helmets strapped
under their chins. Down to the pool's bottom they sank,

then struggled to the surface. Some sputtered and let
go their rifles, but most somehow managed to cross
to the other side, fighting the water, threshing and bobbing.

There were so many young men along with a few women
I did not at first recognize as such that the waters soon
churned and the scene reminded me of the D-day invasion

when some survived to charge the beachhead across sand
while others gave their blood to the surf. Watching all this
I felt that I too was walking on water, but lucky to wear only

a bikini, have no officer yelling in my face, and no nation
waiting to be liberated, occupied, or given the gift of democracy.
And I rejoiced that I had no children to send to the sacrifice.

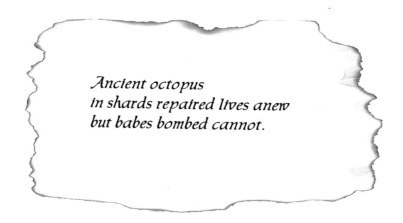

*Ancient octopus
in shards repaired lives anew
but babes bombed cannot.*

APPOINTMENT IN SAMARRA

"An appointment in Samarra"
meant that you could not
fool Mr. Death, that you
flew to Samarra to avoid
him in Paris or Chicago,

but ran into him there
where all along he intended
to find you, had planned it
from day one. I find
Samarra on the map now,

not far from the Tigris
and Euphrates, the lazy
rivers of Eden, where
Mr. Death has much help
fulfilling his quota.

THE INEVITABLE ▲▼▲

— After Mark Bahti

There is a Pueblo Indian story about a man
who was so disrespectful of life
that a snake he had offended killed him.

But his spirit was summoned back
to face the village elders, who were sad
for all the harm this man had done on earth

and all the good he had failed to do.
"Sorrow lay on their hearts because this man
had not believed nor lived with a good heart."

At last the man who had been disrespectful
of so much life began to share the sorrow.
By such a tale we may know what is ahead

for someone we know, though not for a time.

A POET OF WORLD WAR I ᴧᵥᴧ

"But perfection is hard to achieve, at least on a battlefield."
— Eugene Wise

Wilfred Owen, in an old Boche dugout
stinking with rats and a corpse beside him

worked at pentameter as if to say
chaos *will* not rule, yet he knew it would.

But Milton and Shakespeare in no-man's land
offered no comfort. Wiser at twenty than others

at eighty, Wilfred saw through lies he would die by,
the infectious disease that begins with words

and spreads through the flesh. To such a poet
all the world should be metaphor, music, and dream

harmless as butterflies that flutter through smoke.
Even in that hell Wilfred longed to revise the text

of landscape, clean up the foulest of foul papers.
Had his pen had the power wasted on cannons

he'd have restored trees that had been shredded
and he'd have willed every horse back on its legs.

Apples and arbors would have reappeared
in his lifetime. After hours of labor he would

with pentameter incise on stone not needed for graves
a poem no soldier could read without putting down

his weaponry. Yet Wilfred left off his pursuit
of poetry and peace, donned his gas mask

and climbed out of the crater to take his place on the line.

ON THE RIM ᴬᵛᴬ

Walking the rim of an ancient volcano
I recall something my old friend Walter Lowenfels said:
Our country survives as a series of craters.

OVER HERE ⚬⚬⚬

Over There, Over There,
it was always Over There,
a tune we knew well
as the soldiers went marching,
traipsed up the gangplank —
off on a Liberty ship,
off to France, off to the Pacific,
off to Vietnam, off to Korea
(the one I'd have died in).
The hawkers told us
we had to have them —
wars unavoidable, wars
that were graded — Good,
Better, and Best. It took
demons and devils to convince
those who desired their sons
to stay on the farm.
Our cities grew upward,
piercing the clouds.
Then one day I woke to my wife
standing beside our bed,
cup of tea trembling in her hand.
"The Trade Towers," she said,
"the airplanes." It was now
Over Here.

A V-MAIL FROM 1942

We'll never know what Herb meant when he concluded,
"That ain't hay!" for these miniature letters,
photographed and reduced to a fourth the size
of the originals, had been censored, the blacked out
passages resembling the pages of a dossier.
There would be no invisible writing, no tricks for spies
to get away with. "The show was hot!" was the way
Herb summed up the battle, all that was left of it.
"We live in pyramidal tents," he explained,
and hinted that the Sphinx was not far away.

Rommel with his genius was chasing after Herb,
racing over the sands with his half-tracks and tanks,
each with a big black swastika. "I've seen Tunis, Bizerta,
Mekinez, and many other hot spots," Herb wrote his wife,
"though not much night life." His style we could call
G.I. Jocular, the cracking hardy manner mandatory
when writing home to wife and kids or mom and pop.

"We swam every day at a lovely beach in the African sun,"
he went on, "and the Sirocco they talk about brings us blasts
of heat unparalleled for me, almost as bad as artillery,
shock waves of it." Herb ended his scrawl with a hope:
"Let me hear from you," and I, who bought this V-mail
at a yard sale for a dollar years later, leave him there,
a soldier crouched in sand, with Rommel out to get him,
sun, wind, and sand unfriendly. "With Love," Herb
signed off, and I imagine that in his life or death
in North Africa he served bravely and honorably.
And so do troops in other wars, but few will outdo
Herb in reducing hell to fit a miniature page.

A REST FROM THE NEWS

Rumi, ever the dreamer, longed for a rest
from the news, and believed the world

should be permitted time out, suffer no new
afflictions. Would not a pause in hostilities

be welcome? No sooner do armed Persians subside
than the Greeks stride forth to battle with each other,

then Rome disrupts the serenity of seas and forests,
and sands of Egypt are seldom given a rest.

Men seem to think any scene is good for a battle.
In Rumi's day the sky was ignored as a source

for news, a resource for war, but new empires
came along with bombers and missiles.

In truth Rumi would not be pleased at the progress
of man's quest for Utopia.

FOUND POEM ᴧᵛᴧ

E.B. White, White Flag, *quoted in*
Alan Armstrong's Spring Journal, *2003*

"We are sorry to see misuse
of the word 'Fascist.'

If we recall matters,
a Fascist is a member

of the Fascist party
or a believer in Fascist

ideals. These are:
a nation founded on

bloodlines, political
expansion by surprise

and war, murder
or detention of un-

believers, transcendence
of state over individual,

obedience to one leader,
contempt for parliamentary

forms, plus some
miscellaneous gymnastics

for the young and
a general feeling of elation."

SCHOLARSHIP
TO THE RESCUE ᴀᴠᴀ

Did Mohammed feed them
the cake of love

or the cake of hate?
That is what the scholars

long to know, pouring
over the Koran, and now

and then taking a look
at the Holy Bible as well.

We are never disappointed.
We always find precisely

what we wish, be it war,
be it peace, be it hate, be it love.

THE RUSH TO THE FINISH ⋏⋎⋏

The words said by Socrates
as he was handed the cup
of hemlock were reported
to be "No need to rush,
for the sun is still striking
the mountains," and his friends
tried one last time
to persuade him to escape,
and they were eager to help,
not to impose the sentence.

But the philosopher did not
choose delay or escape.
The shadows advanced
and the poison worked its way
as he may have reflected
that those to come after
would pay little heed
to what wisdom he left
and that therefore it made
no sense to leave a bit more.

Thus do our philosophers,
encouraged by those who heed
them not, abandon us,
leave us to tyrants and fools.

THE HOMERIC PROPORTIONS ⅄ᵧ⅄

Tommy Franks is in charge, so surely
this is a chummy war, as if conducted

by schoolyard pals, and with experience
as a manager of a baseball team Bush

is the right man to see that the war
is regarded as a game — and as a signer

of death warrants in Texas he got
experience that now comes in handy.

When he mocked another Born Again
Christian for begging for her life just

before her execution, we should
have noted what we were dealing with —

another cold-blooded killer, his compassion
reserved for his own. The daughters

of others he sends off to war. The daughters
of others go to prison for drug offenses

and drunk driving, youthful indiscretions.
Yet strangely this man who has benefited

all his life from special treatment is against
affirmative action.

THE TOMB OF
THE UNKNOWN SOLDIERS ▲▼▲

*"Go forth under the open sky and list
to Nature's teachings."*
— William Cullen Bryant, "Thanatopsis"

The marble is polished and perfect,
a block hewn from the Rockies,
image of the unspoiled and virginal,
white as unsullied snow, and tourists
come to admire it, sitting with crossed
knees as if in a trance of adoration.

But alas, this stone has developed a crack
as if an earthquake has attacked
or a tired, creaky voice — indignant perhaps —
has cried out from within. In panic a new
block of marble is ordered. Let it be hewn
at great public expense, and make sure
it is flawless and unsullied and kept silent
lest we hear it speak with groans and creaks
and cries to the wind regarding the dead.

THE BIRDS OF IRAQ ᴀᵞᴀ

No more a bird of paradise, this cormorant
stumbles like a drunk or black-caped wraith
out of the lapping oil and in his last
wobbling stand he glares at us as if to ask

why we have done this. And then he falls,
his wings in an instant embedded as if
in gleaming coal for untold eons or etched
on a city's ebony gate with striding kings

and lions. This bird flew ancient skyways
where Alexander conquered yet left birds
alone, did not purloin their sky. You might
conclude that Eden means a land of death,

not love for those above, below, and in between.

WHITE CLOUDS FOR BUDDHA △▽△

— *After Thubten Jigme Norbu's* Tibet Is My Country

1.
Familiar with your kind from past lives
mountains greet you anew.
But you've forgotten their names
and how they warned you, no climbs allowed!

2.
With enough sadness to last a lifetime
the abandoned child observes new faces,
seeking just one who might tell the truth.
And no toy will suffice for distraction!

3.
Silver poplars of foothills give way to cedars.
Even so the spirit opens a path to the heights.
One leaf of wisdom is enough for this life.
White clouds offer cushions for Buddha.

4.
Monks chanting — Oh, most welcome music
freely given to mountains and valleys.
And if invaders would unblock their ears
they would hear prayers that can never be silenced.

5.
In hours that should be devoted to sorrow
we put on bold faces and fly bloody flags.
But how long can silk ripple in the wind?
It is best to donate at least one tear to the river of grief.

6.
How the dying man pities them, those
he leaves behind who must still suffer.
He gestures with sad eyes.
If only he could leave them Nirvana!

FORGIVENESS ▲▼▲

— *After the Korean*

Mountain wind, a cricket crying,
a tavern where three roads cross.

All is healed between us. Without
a word we speak of old times.

The war is not to be undone,
but feel free, my friend, to claim

that you're the one who won.
Oh yes, the hearth fire's hot

and we cannot sit here all night.

SNOW ON SNOW, SAND ON SAND ▲▼▲

— After Thubten Jigme Norbu's Tibet Is My Country

A soldier told a reporter that after his first
battle — call it that — he found killing
to be fun and he is grateful
for the wonderful toys we taxpayers
provide. Perhaps, then, we should think
of ourselves as the parents of soldiers
at play, and arms makers as toy merchants.

Perhaps that soldier enjoyed the same
sport in a previous life and has forgotten
the names of his playmates, friend and foe.
Past lives may come down to this:
just doing the same damn things over and over.

Addiction means repeating mistakes
for a lifetime and not learning anything.
Therefore for men and nations life after life
may show nothing but a lack of progress
and failure of mentors and gurus to speak up
and challenge devotion to lies and illusion.

Mountains, ever watchful, may be mentors
and offer advice, but in tongues
that can be mistaken for a rise in the wind
or more snow on snow to the point of avalanche.

What chance does a lost leaf of wisdom
have when afloat in white clouds?
And in the midst of battle what man stops
to listen for what a chant or lost prayer may say?

IN ANY LANGUAGE,
ANY TEMPLE ▲▽▲

— for Amritjit Singh

In the Sikh temple my friend
translates the chant for me:

"You can choose to give
or not to give, but you have

everything." These words
are addressed to God

by these believers, but I
hear it as if God speaks,

or the guru who wrote:
"You can have it all,

but that does not mean
monkeys will not caper

on your grave." Why
do we not bless monkeys

who caper on our graves
or cavort in the ashy air,

and why cling to anything
but blessings and our

ability to give them?
If that's what we want

of God, should we not
do likewise, abundantly?

WAR CRIMES ◢◥◣

A killer of ninety-nine victims
asked the guru if he could be saved,
spared from hell. The guru gazed
benignly over the crowd and said,
"Forgiveness requires a very very
good deed indeed. Do you have
any idea what that could be?"

"Well," said the supplicant,
"the reason I ask is that tonight
I plan to pick my hundredth victim.
Will I be saved if I stay home
and read a good book? Would that
be good enough for salvation?"

The guru said that it would not.
Later, in court, the killer claimed
the guru should be charged
with all the murders after and
including the one hundredth.
"One kind word from him and
I would not have killed more,
and by now I might be a good man."

Even so the arguments run.
Great men tire of their crimes,
then demand credit for those
they did not get around to committing.

OUT OF THE SILENCE
IN A QUAKER MEETING

On First Day a man stood up and said
"Our task, Friends, is to be worthy
of what we were spared for!" That's all

the man said, and failed to explain what
he had in mind or provide any context.
I have heard lines like that in the street

or in bars, and assumed they were uttered
by those who were half insane, perhaps
some bearded fool muttering to himself.

But then again, there might be a context
one does not speak of, for it's odd how
life and light waver, how one is spared

or is not — the diagnosis outlived or war
survived or the dread nuclear nightmare
delayed far beyond probabilities although

there is nothing on earth not hostage still.
The man rose to his feet on First Day —
a morning that had somehow arrived

as promised, grace enough. But another
war was in progress and each day's evil
more than sufficient to balance its blessings.

OIL ᴧᴦᴧ

Oil for the sputtering mower
which each weekend makes me clamp my skull
with both hands and scream like the woman
on the bridge in Munch's woodcut, "The Scream" —
all for a carpet-sized lawn!

Oil for the weed-eater which works almost as well
as a scythe. Oil for the leaf-blower, strapped
on the back like a flame-thrower. Oil for black tires
we still cart to the landfill, a few gallons
locked inside each. They become a black hill,

shift around like the coaltips of England.
Oil for the van tugging the boat
and for all the jet skis racing, ripping
across yacht bows, our lake crisscrossed and laced
and the fumes hanging low like perfumed fog.

Oil for the supersonic jets which blasted
the ozone, shaved hours off a trip for a few.
For them we let worms eat holes in earth's skull.
And above all oil for the car big as a whale,
lurching through smog, its genial ochre-gold breath

turning our skies into sewers. Oil for the dune
buggies and three-legged bikes breaking backs
of reptiles, who survived millions of years
only to perish like this. Oil for plastic —
for the spoon used once and tossed out — to endure

until Doomsday. Oil for Plexiglas covers
on food trays. Oil for the diapers which capture
the coprolite, which will still be there
for the archaeologist of the year 5000 A.D.
if there is such a person. Oil, say my children,

for demolition derbies, for tractor pulls,
for pure speed, oil for sloshing
on the marijuana heaped up, burned in an orgy
of righteousness. Oil to ship Vermont jelly
to California, California jelly to Vermont.

Oil for Air Force One — to impress and depress.
Oil for tanks, planes and ships plowing on.
And for black ink to print words etched in thin oil.
Oil for the poems — odes for and against war for oil.
                              And oil for the elegies.

TROPHIES ᴧᵥᴧ

In other wars the collecting of trophies was common —
heads, bags of ears, scalps, not to mention genitalia.

But none of our heroes today will have the bad taste
to take one polished skull back to the White House,

hand it across, snap a salute, and report to the President,
                              "Mission Accomplished!"

BLOOD FOR OIL ▲▼▲

*"It is only the very foolish who do
not believe the obvious."*
— Oscar Wilde

What we stand for
all too soon becomes
what we put up with,

first the making
routine the dying
and killing,

then censorship if
we wish to know
all that is done in

our names or if we
want to honor
the fallen by reciting

their names as
the mission each
day becomes all

the more mysterious
for its lack of
justification. First

this, then that excuse
is cited, then proved
mendacious. No one

seems to have noticed
that oil executives
are running the war.

A three-letter word
is, I assume, simply
too obvious. Dot

by dot the foolish
take their bloody
time connecting.

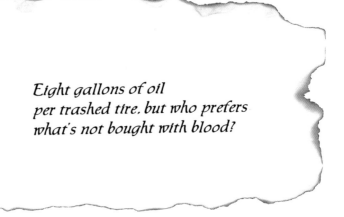

Eight gallons of oil
per trashed tire, but who prefers
what's not bought with blood?

INVASION OF MIND ▲▼▲

War's at the window,
is bound to get in.

In through the window
and right through the door,

in through the pipelines
and right through the wires.

War's in the air, no need
to plug in. Not one brain

cell is left uninvaded, not
one good mood unshattered.

Thrown on the lawn,
hawked through the news,

war can't help but get in.
Then how, my dear Friend,

do we get our brains back?
Soaked in war, minds

have been ravaged. We
are all raped by this war.

Tell your mind to get well,
begin telling it now, for

it will take years, many years.

WAR AS CONSTANT

I opened the history book
which said the English
were ready for the attack
though the French were not.

It said I am Carlyle
and the mobs are about
to rush the Bastille.
It said the redskins

are hiding behind
pecan trees in America.
It said the immortal work
will outlast the outcome,

whichever side wins.
It said the best weapons
have not yet been perfected
but the ones we have will

do fine to make history.
It said Joan of Arc
was a sensitive maiden
but stirred up a fool war.

It said Einstein not yet.
It said Ach, this bomb
has changed everything
except man. It said

millions are driven
like cattle, their value
irrelevant to their fate.
It said all earth

is an abattoir. It said
Nevermore. It said
That's what they all said.
It said our war is to end

all war. Always, it said,
Nevermore. Never again.
That's what they said,
what they say, what we say.

MINE FIELDS ▲▾▲

In more than one land now
peasants herd children
in front of their sheep,

for they can afford
to lose children but not
sheep. But if you think

they do not weep
for these children you are
as mistaken as those

who believe these wars
are for causes more noble
than gold, oil, or ego.

SCORCHED PAGES ᴬ ᵛᴬ

"And thus the empire is maintained."
— Ezra Pound

"Genocide" debated
while children die, women raped,
thus empires maintained.

Lies so far from truth
that coast-to-coast offers not
nearly room enough.

Am I seeing things?
I'd swear Pinocchio's nose
appeared on that face.

News of one thousand
dead in Iraq reaches us
on our son's yahrzeit

Everything burning
said Buddha. Best not look, then,
over horizon.

A KIND OF SOLUTION

"The barbarians were a kind of solution."
— Cavafy

Is that the view we are asked to adopt?
— that we, the barbarians, have brought
a solution, no need to wait for decay,
the crumbling of houses and walls, the dying
of generations that — if allowed to be born —
would only bring the myriad problems
known to ancient kingdoms and empires?

Let us take the long view, look at the gains,
First of all, there will be no need to grieve
for what and whom are not there. Some day
we will be thanked for the gift of chaos
as soon as it has advanced to numb oblivion.

Without our bombs, bullets and other wise
weapons all too much that is imperfect
and flawed might thrive. Think of the cracks
in the walls of the mosques, the bad skin
of women, not to mention the sins evaded.

What we have brought to this land once
called Babylon could be called Nirvana,
but that term, our experts tell us, is Buddhist,
and when we bring solutions we must beware
of cultural delicacies lest we bomb the wrong land.

ANTHROPOLOGY ◢◣

A Tibetan woman giggled
as the Nazi researchers
with calipers and tape measures
scurried about, took careful
notes regarding her nose,
broad cheekbones, tilt of neck.
They mapped her skull
as a butcher does beef.

They patted clay on her face
to collect an impression
to take back to Berlin where,
along with others of inferior
races, she would be displayed
in their museum proving
that Aryans are best and most
beautiful. All these efforts
were filmed for cinema news
as researchers went about
their work all over the globe.

It seemed that inferior faces
were everywhere, gazing out
of bright eyes, just waiting
to be measured and collected.
It was amazing how many
inferior races those scholars
could find. But had the Tibetan
known what they had in mind,
she might not have giggled
so much, thus confirming yet
another conclusion already
reached, which was that inferior

persons and peoples were far
more prone to laughter. Charlie

Chaplin was yet another example,
for who but a very inferior fellow
would laugh at a dictator so great
that he could spin the globe
on his index finger, though not for long?

Sandstorms — bad enough —
but add war to make heroes —
war zones of Eden.

A CONFESSION

Let's admit it. Like parents
with spoiled children
we are proud of how well

our officials can lie,
how deftly the syllables
roll off their tongues,

how impeccably, pro-
fessionally. And the best
liar of all holds his nation

in thrall because he can lie
and lie and lie and lie some
more while we look on amazed

and then hand him his allowance.

HANDS

"I hate my hands,"
said the surgeon in Iraq,
knowing they did more harm
than good, moving from gut
to gut without half
of what was needed —
not even soap
in their repertoire.

And yet he had to try,
did he not, after the warriors
had done their best,
their level best, their bloody best
—

though a few might one day
                hate their hands.

LAS MANOS ▲▼▲

"Odio mis manos,"
dijo el cirujano en Irak,
sabiendo que hacían más daño
que bien al moverse de tripa
en tripa sin la mitad
de lo que necesitaban —
ni siquiera jabón
en su repertorio.

Y sin embargo tenía que tratar,
verdad, después de que los guerreros
habían hecho lo imposible,
su mejor esfuerzo, el más encarnizado —

aunque algunos quizá algún día
                    odiarían sus manos.

—Translated by Lilvia Soto

THE HOLLOW MEN ▲▼▲

sometimes remind me of children at play
who don't stop to think how they hurt others,

and besides, the hurting and killing is far away
and they never have to look at blood

and realize that it's red just like their own.
Children in such situations take one good look

at this evidence and run in the other direction,
vowing never again to play in such messy ways.

Thus children, it seems, are smarter than leaders,
for they change their behavior as soon as they see

that no one can win when playing such games.
But a leader deaf to all reason and immune

to compassion, who won't look at bodies
or coffins or go near a service for those

he has sent to their deaths, a man who orders
his people not to honor the fallen by speaking

their names or showing portraits from yearbooks
and albums, must be treated as if he is high

on a pedestal, a statue of bronze to be toppled
like any tyrant, and revealed to be equally hollow.

Why do we tolerate such hollow men and allow
them to govern our nations by whim? Is it because

we are too damned embarrassed to stand with a sign
insisting that one by one these hollow men resign?

Think of it, how with far less effort than it takes
to assure a legacy of woe these same hollow men

could have followed laws that create a peaceable kingdom.

THE RETURNEES ▲▼▲

Their lungs are half sand.
Lies leave their brains far too late.
Then one war's enough.

IMAGES ⋏⋎⋏

We avoid TV for a week,
come back to it,
nothing but propaganda.

The network reports
could be scripted
in the Pentagon, most likely

have been. A girl soldier
holds a child in her arms,
a small child with casts

on both legs, since she
was wounded when
both parents were killed.

The soldier rocking
the child in her arms
and the reporter discuss

how glad the Iraqis
are to see the Americans,
the rescuers, the liberators.

First make an orphan
out of the child,
then comfort her.

Way to go — the new
American way, the old
Roman way, Saddam's way.

APRIL FOOLS AFIRE ⋏⋎⋏

I.

"Our tigers drink milk," Szymborska
wrote in a poem which I was reading

when *Democracy Now* gave a report
about killing civilians in Iraq.

In Vietnam our tigers also drank milk,
our soldiers drawn from the best

and gentlest of our boys, though I recall
a G.I. saying "I had to shoot that gook lady

because she might have had a grenade
in her basket." Our soldiers today

are also presumed to have drunk milk.
They are rosy-cheeked and only gradually,

reluctantly, with much encouragement
and many orders, learn to be war criminals.

II.

On National Public Radio a poet reads
a poem about the bombing of Warsaw

and the interviewer quickly replies,
"But that's not an anti-war poem, is it?"

He assures her it is not. And then
he reads a poem about camellias.

Keep poems gentle. Keep them generic,
for war is no longer to be slandered.

It cannot be a good poem if it is anti-war.
We must be gentle these days with the word,

for war is fragile and might die if faith is lost in it.

III.

"These irksome little nations, thick as flies,"
wrote Szymborska in "Voices,"
a poem addressed to Roman emperors.

"If only they weren't always in the way...
but they always do get in the way
with their noxious customs, backward laws,

ineffectual gods." The President's advisers
must know this poem, though perhaps
they did not read it as the poet intended,

for it seems to have inspired them to take on
God knows how many more swarms.
Syria, Iran, North Korea are mentioned

as possible next targets. Yet the poet warned
emperors: "the farther you go, the more there are ...
these pitiable little nations that require supervision

because of their foolish ways ... you just can't
take on all the flies." She added that even
the greatest of empires has to end somewhere.

Szymborska knew that a tour of the spots where
worlds ended could not be completed in a lifetime,
but starting from home we could all view a few.

OF PRESIDENTS & EMPERORS ᴀᵛᴀ

Comparing our imperial leader today to Nero,
whose troops were also engaged in occupation
of Parthian lands along the Euphrates, with about
the same luck as today, we surely must temper
our judgments, forgive a few lies and lives lost,
give thanks that most of the deaths are uncounted,
and not ours. After all, our leader did not murder
his mother. He and she are on excellent terms.

Nero murdered his wife Octavia, also Poppaea,
his second, by kicking her while she was pregnant
with his child, guaranteed divinity. In Washington
you see no such abominations. The lies are genteel
and murder is at the far end of Pathfinders,
Tomahawks, gun ships and Patriot missiles.
Back home we can thank our stars that tribunes
and freed gladiators do not arrive bearing swords
and platters for heads. And because Congress
consists of the deferential they would never be at risk.
Our leader needs not assassinate sassy senators.

He would never set fire to Washington or build
an ostentatious mansion like Nero's over the ruins.
As a God-fearing Christian he would never thank
Jupiter for throwing javelins of fire at his enemies,
nor would he go on tour to read his poems or play
his harp in the provinces. Yet for his speeches
our President gets as much applause as Nero,
whose soldiers prodded those who nodded off.

In the Oval Office no visitor is obliged to fall upon
knees and weary the President's hand with kisses.
Yet the fear Tacitus expressed could be voiced today.
He worried that such "a monotony of disasters"

as those ordered by Nero might, if recited, disgust all
who heard them. He preferred not to sicken his readers
lest they be "fatigued of mind and paralyzed with grief."
In Rome thousands like us could only pray for relief.

THE EXCITEMENT ▲▼▲

"They are very excited as they look up
at the planes," said the breathless reporter

of the civilians as bombing progressed
during "shock and awe" for "liberation"

was on its way as it was on D-day.
And of course they were excited,

the citizens of Iraq — scared out of their wits
as they awaited their liberation from life.

Propaganda, as Orwell told us, is a fascinating industry.

PROPAGANDA

The lovely white hospital ship waits offshore,
stocked with miraculous medicines,

and the theme of rescue is resonant
like music over shimmering waters.

Dear boys, your wounds will be dressed
and nurses will offer bosomy comfort.

But there is no mention of how many
body bags are stored in the hold,

each the size of one fallen warrior.
Not far from this scene Florence Nightingale

bent over the dying from another campaign
called Gallipoli.

MANNA FROM HEAVEN ⋏⋎⋏

As if to harvest mushrooms
children grab at parachutes

left on the sands. Some good,
it seems, may yet come of war —

a tent or a garment for a mother,
or perhaps a few needed shrouds.

REMEMBERING THE SIXTIES ⋏⋎⋏

In London as U.S. planes were bombing
Cambodia I felt obliged
to say that not all Americans approved.

"That's all right, dear," said the waitress,
"Somebody's got to keep the wogs down.
But woe to us when we are reborn as wogs!"

DEMONOLOGY ◂▾◂

You say we should not demonize our President,
and that is true.

But you mistake me, for I wish him well,
and great happiness

on his vast ranch in Texas. The bluebonnets
will be in bloom

and many will visit to pay homage to him,
the retired President,

and his library will go up. And believe me,
I make no jokes

about that, for Laura is a librarian and can take
on the task of arranging

all of them, including the ones her husband
might yet get around

to reading in the pleasant retirement I wish him.
In fact, it is my prayer.

SADDAM'S BURROW ▲▼▲

He is bearded and dazed from weeks on the run,
days in his burrow not far from the river,
in sight of one of his palaces on the opposite bank,
but this Saddam is no longer the swimmer he was

as a young assassin. And alas, that palace
has been taken over by Americans. The homeless
man must be content with his burrow, and perhaps
it would be best just to leave him there. In truth

I doubt if this man with lice in his hair is the great
Saddam. I think he may be Kafka's underground
man, who also lived in a burrow. Like Saddam,
that fellow had countless enemies who sought him

incessantly, and from underground he heard all night
the scratching of claws and endured horrific smells.
Yet he knew he must not draw attention to his burrow,
which — like Saddam's — was covered with a flap

of turf. Kafka's man, like Saddam, awoke with a rat
nibbling his nose. But Kafka, unlike those who rejoice
at this dictator's capture, knew that you cannot seek
a foe deep in a burrow without digging one for yourself.

ENTANGLED WITH LIES △▽△

"We seek truth in a chaos of lies."
— Judy Ray

Like Laocoön with the python
wrapped around him, these men —

and women too — are strangled
by their lies — coiling, rarely

relenting — one falsehood
after another, each more facile

than the last. Our National
Security Advisor with her

tricky tongue tossed off
one glib fib after another.

 "Oh, yes, they have jars
on their shelves with both

chemical and biological
weapons in them." Was she

inspired, I wondered,
by some auntie's cellar

with its shelves of strawberry
preserves and green tomatoes?

The lies are canned too, fester
like botulism. "COLLATERAL

DAMAGE," says the label,
but what's in that jar?

MOVIE REVIEW ᴀᵥᴀ

The charges against
Michael Moore's movie
called *Fahrenheit 9/11*
included the following:
It was not fair to show
happy Iraqis in Baghdad
the day of the bombing —
especially since for many
of them it was their last
day on earth, their
last meal, and so on.

And Moore had no proof
that the oil men schemed
for a pipeline through
Afghanistan and so on.
And talk about cheap shots!
Zooming in on the President
while his face was twitching
and he was adjusting his tie
just before he told the world
he had ordered a new round
of Shock and Awe — greater
and grander than what
he unleashed on Afghanistan —
a spectacular show of fireworks —
death being so distant
and abstract that there would be
no need to count bodies, a great
disappearing act, and magic
to assure re-election
in the strangest of worlds yet.

THE MINISTRY
OF PROPAGANDA ᴀᵛᴀ

Retired generals in various cities
are interviewed nightly about the war.

The maps are shown and strategies
discussed with great enthusiasm.

Our troops are grabbing the bulls
by their horns. Resistance is soon

to be overcome. But resistance
to what is never quite defined.

The news anchors gaze upon
these guests with the admiration

until now shown only to movie stars.
There are no views represented

other than this gung-ho enthusiasm
for war. From every military base

intelligence and publicity personnel
fan out to offer their services to media

as part-time advisers and experts.
They explain and make palatable

all the President's policies, e.g.,
allowing no photos of flag-draped

coffins bound for Arlington or home
town cemeteries, though it would be

hard to find one that has not added
a few from overseas to its holdings.

Every technique described by Orwell
or practiced by Goebbels is in place,

but so far few have dared say so.

THE MINISTRY OF TRUTH ◢◤◢

That we have agreed to use such terms,
that we have been taught them,
that we now say *ethnic cleansing*,
that we now say *collateral damage*,
that we conceptualize in Newspeak,
that we have become numbed,
is a judgment on all of us.

We should have refused to be taught,
we should never have mouthed
such obscenities. We should not
have taken the edge off, blunted
the bloody knives of speech.

And when we are cleansed
and when we are collateral
and when we are nameless
targets of *anti-personnel* weaponry,
and when we are utterly consumed,
and when we are red rain,
and when we are ash, then
may someone set the truth free,
scream it out – truth in all
its horrors. Let it be naked,
obscene, real, not to be glossed over,
not to be sweetened. Let no one
say "the horror is that there is
no horror." Let the horror
be known, that it may die of exposure
even as the last dragon is slain.

PATRIOTS ▲▼▲

Only one miss in over forty, the public was told
when it looked like the Patriot missiles were saving

Israel from Saddam Hussein's attacks. But in fact
those Patriots were blowing up in the night sky

all by themselves, their accuracy not the ninety-
some percent stated, but less than ten.

They were a worthless weapon in that first
of the Iraq wars, though sometimes far worse,

since they also shot down British and American
planes with so-called friendly fire. Still,

the Patriot missile is the Pentagon's darling,
and when an official is asked why, he says

there's a lot of money involved, the contracts
are in the billions and benefit some of our

best corporations. He names them.
Proud names. Subsidized. Prestigious.

THE WONDER WOMAN
OF AEROSPACE ᴧᵛᴧ

What a wonder is this woman who is profiled
in the paper! How well-rounded, how high-tech,

how efficient and proficient as she sits behind
her desk where ranged before her are her children —

not the teens she has at home, but the products
of her work place. They are only toys, of course,

for the real things would break through her desk
and might blast away the building. These cute

maquettes are mockup versions of the missiles
and many kinds of weapons that she oversees

and sells to all who can afford them. She is a lady
C.E.O., a woman of the year, an arms merchant

par excellence. She trots around the globe, earns
a million frequent flyer miles each year. She is

a leader who rolls up her sleeves and digs into
each detail. She attends to any project that may

earn a profit, win a war, or have a one in a thousand
chance of hitting an incoming missile with her missile.

She is a star of industry, a patriot, and more, and yet
is also humble, modest, self-effacing, and when at home

is glad to help her husband cook. Her climb to the top
is quite inspiring, though she will not toot her own horn

but refer you to her publicist. A rude reporter asked her
if she ever dreams of children blown apart or women

like herself turned into bloody litter. "My goal," she said,
is excellence — I have a job and someone has to do it."

But now and then we wonder why.

AFTER THE BATTLE

The choice is so clear.
More Propaganda or Grief.
We know which they choose.

FUTILITY ᴀᴠᴀ

From a letter a soldier wrote as he grieved
a friend he saw die I extract these words:
"We have no business being over here
anymore and most of the men around me
feel the same way. As soon as we leave
it will be a civil war here and mass chaos,
no matter how long we stay here. I think
it is important that people back home
know how we that are here feel about
this bullshit war." But the soldier may not
have laid down his arms in protest or sent
the same letter to the President, since all
soldiers know full well that this President
heeds no such complaints, and rarely reads.

TWO DADS ⋀⋁⋀

When George Bush was asked
if, before he ordered Shock
and Awe, he had asked his father
for advice, he pointed up
and replied that he took orders
not from his earthly father
who lives out in Texas, but
the other one high above.

The motto *Gott Mitt Uns*
adorned Nazi stilettos and belts.
Hitler shared his Eagle's Nest
with his dogs and the god Thor.
Caligula was often absent
from Rome because he communed
at his mountain retreat
with his brother god Jupiter.

At night I stroll out
and chat with kingly Orion
but he gives me not a clue
as to whether he's my real dad
or where to send my bombers.

IN PURSUIT OF THE ABSTRACT ᴧ ᵥᴧ

*"The personal interpretation of the abstract
is the only reality."*
— Michael Annis

We are invited to tour an exhibition of landscapes
at the Museum of Art, and since we daily search
for serenity, a peaceable land, green gentle hills,
I am happy to scan a number of scenes delightful
and appealing. I'd be glad to move into that desert
or valley with the lone house, and then I spot
a painting by the late and great Bruce McGrew.

But alas, there's a skull in the sky of his painting —
horse or cow or goat, I'm not sure — and I turn away
from this white bone to look down over a wall
to see an amazing creation. Dangling from wires
are skeletons flying or cavorting through the air,
a scene from the Day of the Dead or All Saints,
and this wild creation distracts because it makes
me think of 9/11, that day of horrors when like
these skeletons of paste and paper falling or flailing
or fleeing through the sky three thousand perished,
though not so lucky as dolls with bones white as ivory
and bloodless. These skeletons were not flung out
as ash and debris nor did they leap singly or hand
in hand. But they are sufficient for reflection regarding
death random, sudden and absurd, and to wonder why
we need bombers and missiles if such creatures ride
the sky already. Is there not enough threat and terror
seen and unseen around and above us? No wonder
we worship the abstract and prefer not to speak or write
of anything but the trivial. Perhaps these skeletons
have something to tell us. Their jaws are open as if
to shout their last words, "Mehr Licht!" or "What

is the Question?" or "Donde va?" or "Wie Gehts?"

And their eye sockets still seem to seek as we do
a peaceable kingdom or a city where Communitas
is in flower. Perhaps they would be willing to return
if we assure them that this time they have nothing to fear.
Let us study white bones, be they a flock of skeletons led
by a horseman or a single skull above a landscape by McGrew.

AFTER TAKAHASHI

—for Lucien Stryk

I.

In the light of explosions
the lovers yelled at the war
to be over so they could get back to work
on the peace. They knew it would be harder.

2.

Five baby birds in a rotten stump yapping
their desperate cries. Next day the nest is empty.
Indict for war crimes the fool who downed the tree,
or the unbelled cat and its Commander-in-Chief.

3.

Kanoko was afraid of flowers for good reason.
More than once they had wounded her.
So she claimed, adding that only God knows
how those blossoms got dipped in blood.

4.

Warplanes back from the killing field,
skimming shadows strafing our back yard,
letting us live. At least for now we are exempted.
How can one cry out, pleading for peace?

5.

He told how his father slipped away, let go
his grip, as if Beethoven's 6th had been composed
just for this, the slipping away. But then he added
that perhaps it was the 8th — the one that brings peace.

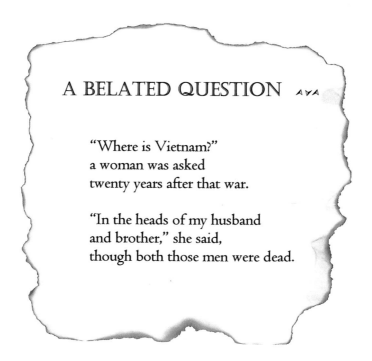

A BELATED QUESTION

"Where is Vietnam?"
a woman was asked
twenty years after that war.

"In the heads of my husband
and brother," she said,
though both those men were dead.

VIETNAM WALL ▲▼▲

What we love is the ambiguity, the relief
we obtain by gazing only upon the back
of the mirror, the unwelcome pictures
reflected away into the other direction,
fading in the red doppler glow of forgetting.
What we love is the thick wall between us
and the unwelcome beholding. What we love
is that we can stand at grave's depth and see
or smell no bodies. What we love is the lack
of fuss, the documents not closely examined,
the history left ambiguous, our grief palatable,
the black as hell surface wiped smooth daily.
What we love is our war brought into focus
for the admiring, a celebration regardless —
a war like a shell gleaming with neither seed
nor explosives inside. What we love is the hollow
heart and the not saying. What we love is the hope,
the numinous names in all their bloodless splendor
as they might have glowed in their long living.
What we love about the black wall shining is that
the war is over, until we climb back up to ground zero.

HARMLESS POEMS,
AN OXYMORON ▲▼▲

> *"Through the Vietnam War, American poets divided the country."*
> — Poetry Consultant, Library of Congress

I still find it easy to recall how we poets cleft
our nation in twain, broke the hearts of mothers,

almost brought down the government by flinging
sonnets through the air, launching sestinas from far

out at sea. Poets torched cities with flamethrower
ghazals and machine gun gathas. The pacifist Stafford,

like the Quaker farmer in *The Friendly Persuasion,*
decided it was time to take up arms and fight fire with fire.

He grabbed his pen and shot off three poems before breakfast
every day, year after year in that long war. He was wounded

by critics with blowpipes, but soldiered on out in Oregon.
The Mississippi River, incidentally, served as our role model.

If it could divide the country, we thought, why couldn't we?
Our tankas rumbled along the expressways, churning out

smog to rival smoke trails left by B-52s. But no matter
how hard we tried we could not get airborne to bring down

those bombers. They kept dropping mother bombs, the kind
that gave birth in mid air to smaller ones. But then the war

ended, and when we poets were asked by Congress how
we could justify the casualties we inflicted with our dime

a line broadsides we quoted the car and tobacco executives
as well as those who ran the war, for in truth their lines

were poetic as well. "When they make a safe car or cigarette
I'll manufacture a harmless poem," said a poet soon found

in contempt of Congress. "Even a Scripto lighter blows up
in people's faces," said another, "so why should my verse

be full of nothing but hot air?" An impassioned admirer
of the ancient poet Sappho pointed out that apples in stores

are more poisonous than the one the wicked queen offered
Snow White. He rolled a Delicious across the green carpet

of the hearing room and called it a found poem.
A guard, perhaps thinking the apple was a grenade,

fell to the floor as he grabbed it. "These proceedings
are adjourned," announced the Senator, "for I will not allow

poets to divide this Congress the way they did this nation."

IN PRAISE OF REFUSENIKS ▲▼▲

All the heroes should have stayed home,
their refusal to fight condemned as cowardice,

and perhaps they would be punished with prison
by those who think they have the rights

to bodies — the bodies of these soldiers ordered
to fight and die — the bodies of distant children

to be destroyed in a flash. Bodies belong
to the leaders, even if they are no wiser than puppets.

The medals are being minted like money.
But what can they buy for a boy in a body bag

or a girl who lost her virginity to a missile?

ANOTHER DAY OF IT ᴀᵛᴀ

A convoy is ambushed, our troops captured,
some killed, the bodies displayed.
Our President says he is "pleased
by progress," but warns that it will be
a longer war than he has often promised.

One soldier goes berserk and lobs
grenades at his comrades. Craters
pock Baghdad where buildings stood
for centuries. One woman captured
has inspired an editorial entitled
"The Pinking of the Armed Forces."

A high priority for the President
is exempting Americans, including
himself, from future prosecution
for war crimes. My essay comparing
this demand to George Washington's
order to his troops warning them
of dire punishment should they
disrespect the enemy in any way
goes unpublished due to the silent,
almost ubiquitous censorship
imposed on American writers
by editors happy to be of service.

Linda Ronstadt is escorted out
of the casino by bouncers for insulting
the President, as if those Hitler days
are back, when comedians were taken
out and shot for joking about Der Führer.
Are we just a few steps away
from repeating those days? Must I expect

the new S.S. to come calling, and will
they kill the dog as Hitler's goon squads
did those who tried to defend their masters?

PRE-EMPTIVE JUDGEMENT ᴧʏᴧ

Saddam dead at last?
Bush gloats as he counts one more
death warrant fulfilled.

INTEGRITY BEYOND CHALLENGE ▲▼▲

*"The opposite of integrity is not dishonesty,
but hypocrisy."*
— Christopher Caldwell

If we as mischievous children
had had such eager defenders
we'd never have been shamed
for our trivial crimes, or received
spankings that left us like dogs
kicked and left out in the cold.

Volunteer word-spinners rise
to defend this man of integrity,
and there is ever a new twist,
since denying his lies no longer
works. The logic of Caldwell
is this: so long as the lies
are sincere and therefore not
hypocritical the integrity is still
intact, halo aglow over the teller.

Caldwell even adapts out of context
words of a philosopher who wrote
that "integrity can ... exist under
the cover of all other vices except
this one," hypocrisy. In any case,
since no one can accuse this liar,
who goes on repeating the lies,
of not being sincere, his claim
to integrity can hardly be challenged.

Neat! Joseph Goebbels could not
have done it better for his Führer.
Sixty years of deconstructive

sophistry, semiotics, and relativism
to the point of denying that any fact
or truth is eternal has led to vast gains
in the art of propaganda. Just move
the words over, realign them, redefine
them, and you can have it your way,
any way, any day, and all for free,
gifts of the volunteer word-spinners,
a great asset for those with integrity.

COWARDICE ⋏⋎⋏

At ninety will I take for my role model
Bertrand Russell as he sat in protest

in Trafalgar Square? Or will I stand
with a sign near the Pentagon or Rocky Flats

or Cheyenne Mountain or outside the gate
at the School of The Americas, no matter

what euphemism might hide its purpose by then?
Most likely not, for I suspect I might still

be watching The History Channel as the camera
inside the Trident submarine follows four men

pledged to launch missiles when given the order.
They will not know which cities will be destroyed

within minutes, for all is TOP SECRET, even
from them, though not from all us TV viewers.

Do we witness a Doomsday Machine or a movie set?
Perhaps all reality is now in doubt, and millions

seem to have accepted the notion of Armageddon
as a goal of foreign policy. Perhaps that awaited event

will turn out to be a TV special, available on all channels.

THE ESSENTIAL DISTANCE

The president halts to adjust
his cravat, stretches his neck
as he admires his re-electable face.

But his collar feels tight
and he craves something stronger
than water, but he gave all that up

with his other boyish indiscretions.
It was boring today, hearing
the generals recite the numbers,

those made public and those not.
Like him the generals presume
to share a cause, one good enough

to overcome a certain nausea,
though nothing like what he might
suffer should he visit a battlefield

still wet with blood and vomit
and see the bodies up close,
with no distance, smelling them —

these men and women who planned
to father and mother children.
They espoused no cause but their own

until this man began ranting.

BEDTIME IN
THE WHITE HOUSE ◢◤◢

Imagine going to sleep
with no grief for them,
those faces so familiar
to all the nation, the day's
losses shown on PBS,
the color portraits
used as a border
in Newsweek, their
survivors interviewed
for the newspapers,
each star on the flag
by now represented.

Imagine no regrets,
even being proud
of it, the cost of
one ranting tantrum
just as Claudius
or Caligula boasted
of achievements
so bloody. After all,
it is a matter of style,
no President so obvious
as Saddam or Stalin.

But why would one
duly or not duly
elected prefer to go
down in the roster
as a mild man, another
Millard Fillmore,

an obscure Milquetoast?
The famous Presidents
are the bloody ones,

the good ones so mild
as not to be recalled
in our nightmares.
In the mirror a smirk
of proud satisfaction
like that of Narcissus
is standard. Better
to have bloody hands
than to have no horrors
recalled in your name.

From AZALEA VARIATIONS ᴀ﹀ᴀ

— After the Korean of Kim So-Wol

I.
You could not hear the blossoms
crushed under your feet,
but to me they were lamenting

6.
Twenty years of scorn yet I did not
get the message until you blew
purple blossoms into my face.

8.
When you leave please go quickly
like a blossom in the brisk wind,
and I will vow the same courtesy.

12.
I'm prepared for that day
of your betrayal. Gifts of azaleas
can no longer deceive me.

19.
With the beauty of such blossoms
human woe must have been banished
for at least a thousand miles around.

22.
How blessed is the azalea
to be spared the whims of war,
yet brave enough to defy the winds

24.
He thought he could capture the blossoms
by hacking down that tree
but he did not harvest even one.

38.
Yes, you can scatter blossoms and beg me
to dance as they fall through the air,
but don't count on me or the breeze.

39.
Stride away in a huff right into the sunset,
but leave me our path of blossoms
as if you stagger away from our battlefield.

40.
Like two estranged lovers our land
has been cleft in twain, but don't forget
that both halves are grieving lovers.

41.
I plan to return to the bare trees,
the rocks and lost lands and ghosts
of our blossoms in the chill wind.

46.
Futile, you say, to look for faces in blossoms,
but you have never suffered such a loss
or you'd examine each one, neglect nothing.

49.
I longed to return home to my own being,
but I never got far without its becoming
yours, our souls entangled like blossoms swirling.

50.
Of course I would know it, that hut where
you await me and on the slope azaleas
do their best to fill the valley with blossoms.

THE EYRIE ᴀᵥᴀ

From the ninety-third floor
of Chicago's tallest
she sees the cars on Lake
Shore Drive as trembling
diamonds and garnets.

Mornings she reports
traffic flow to friends,
gridlock on most days.
And when clouds
close in she calls
downstairs to ask
the doorman
if it is raining.

At night she is dazzled
by stars, but awakes
from dreams of a plane
zooming in toward
her living room.
She checks to see
that nothing's
been disturbed.
And yet she stays
because the life aloft
reminds her of how
it would be to live
like angels, leaving
the crass and vulgar
world below.

This is Chicago,
she tells herself —
no need to fear
far from the war
and high in the air,
a mile from Skid Row.

NEIGHBORHOODS ▲▼▲

No village is so small as to lack casualties.
Unseeing eyes in rubble and ash are in fashion.

Schools are converted to morgues, churches
to scenes for firefights. Tanks rumble along,

shake the earth, fire at will, level an apartment
building here, a house there. Children strap

explosives to their chests with the help of fathers,
even mothers. To think all this was brought about

by Mars or Satan is tempting, yet we know
it is ordinary men who in their banality manage it.

We do not even have to leave our neighborhoods
to find those who approve this chaos with all their hearts.

THE VIEWING ◢▼◢

"a little residue of nothing"
—Carolyn Forché

At Niagara the viewers gaze through a waterfall,
imperceptibly less than it was yesterday
or one moment ago

    and the Grand Canyon
is gaping before us although no one can say
whether stone or river will conquer

and in Manhattan a platform has been erected
for the viewing of debris, so that we
may queue up to gaze at the abyss

through a great fall of ash, thinner each day.
Some say this is only a mist of the past
but they are deceived,

    for this is the bloody rain.

TEACHING IN JUVENILE JAIL

". . . but their eyes stayed dead
and I left feeling I might've helped them
if I had tried a little harder."
—Philip Schultz

I too should have tried harder, stayed
a while longer. Only two of the boys
had already killed, and with great effort
I might have deterred the others
from that kind of future. But they say
peers are the best teachers, and those two
who were killers were far more effective
than I as they shared tips with the others.
"Never leave a witness," one said,
"that's the best advice I ever got in my life."
As co-teacher a thirteen-year-old added
that we should "make sure to put the gun
barrel right down on their eyeballs."

When the news about Abu Ghraib
struck home I thought of that jail,
how well advanced its staff was
in methods of shaming and torture.
Grim guards did not hesitate to knock
a kid silly if he got insolent. One
Goddamn or Motherfuck could get
a boy cuffed and tied backwards
on a chair, his knees tucked under.
I spoke up, but to no avail, just
made matters worse. "Are they
always that bad?" I asked my
supervisor and she thought I meant
the boys, not the guards. Therefore
I flunked myself and dropped out

of Juvenile Jail though I still wish
I had taught them to recite "Ulalume"
or "Annabelle Lee" or "The Raven."

But a week later
Saddam's back and Osama
has wandered away.

GUILT ▲▼▲

Each little gesture I question,
seldom rest from gleaning
as if shattered glass dug out
of rubble might still offer
wine worth the drinking,
though it may have held poison.

Whether the sins sought
were those of omission
or commission matters not.
I assess blame for the least
hurt I might have inflicted
with a word. At confession
of evil within I have few
rivals as a priest no doubt
could confirm. "This man,"
he would say, "wears a hair
shirt and rarely comes in out
of the cold. More than once
he has sentenced himself
to death, only at the last
minute offered a stay, which
may run out at any moment."

Yet I am asked to pardon
those who glibly send others
to their deaths. I am asked not
to inquire into their motives.
I am told to vote for them,
to be a forgiving citizen, one
of their fortunate subjects,
and as a believer, although
a convert, keep my silence.

CODA ▲▼▲

"Hey, Hey, L.B.J., how many kids did you kill today?"
Protest chant during the Vietnam War

No one today is trying to exorcise or levitate the Pentagon,
and protesters are not shouting "Hey! Hey! Dubya, Dubya,

how many kids did you kill today?" The dead and wounded
flown back from Iraq arrive in the night with no press coverage,

for citizens must not be disturbed by the sight of so many coffins.
The media are happy to censor themselves, anything to curry

favor with The White House. The numbers of the wounded
are seldom mentioned and the word "hurt" is often used, for it

is softer, as if our young men and women come back with mostly
scratches and bruises. The dead are quietly interred, joining

the fallen from the other good wars, but would it not be appropriate
to entomb them in the White House or bury them in the Rose Garden?

MEDIA WONDERS ▲▼▲

Every time they report that the U.S. did this or that
or said this or that I feel very offended,
indignant, for they do not mean the U.S. did this
or that (although the U.S. may have done this or that
or perhaps has done this or that unfortunate act
because George W. Bush said it or ordered it done).
But let's get one thing straight, Mr. and Mrs. Media,
when you say the U.S. did this or said that
and you really mean Mr. Bush, just say George
W. Bush said or did it and do not implicate us
in his crimes — those of us who hate war and love
wilderness, those of us who want future generations
to have medical care and education and no mountains
of debt and pollution to crawl through. Thanks.

MAKING FREE ᴧᵛᴧ

"there is a way of making free with the past."
Eavan Boland

A wise woman said there's a way
of making free with the past,
that History has little to do
with The Past. And not much
of what I recall resembles
quite the way I remember it.
A vocalic inflection alone
changes what takes place
in the bone. Most is left out,
and like others, I am an un-
reliable witness, maker of myth.

History is written by winners.
History is written by hacks
in service to those in command
as long as they can. History
is erasure, deletion, air brush,
and just plain leaving out
for reasons of taste or not
to offend or because you don't
know half what you claim to.

Sometimes the historian makes
a simple decision not to get
murdered or fired, his or her
bread and butter denied. History
is what is passed on, lifted
from one book to fatten another.

The plagiarist is rarely exposed,
and few reading or hearing
give much of a damn, for already

they know most of it's lies.
Who really believes Oswald
killed Kennedy? Who really
believes Dad was at fault while
Mom was the saint enshrined
in the myth she designed?

Ask anyone you know — start
with grandmother if she's extant.
Ask her to say how it was, really
was, and not leave anything out.
And you'll see that she too is just
another Historian. A few years
go by and you renew the request.

And get a new version, as varied
as that extolled in a story called
Rashomon. Is it possible that each —
involved or eye-witness — beheld
events in at least three ways,
making nine versions, then later
added another before they got
utterly confused, lost in deceptions
until self was the most deceived?

Later they add new variations
as afterthoughts re-solve a crime,
although too late for the man who
went to death row. And thanks
to the deconstructionist scholar
yet a new twisted tale becomes
fact, requiring a new edition

of The Warren Report, or
the latest on global warming
or the birth of a planet already
ten or a thousand light years old.

The most popular drug to prevent
heart attacks turns out to be sure
to thicken the plaque and provoke

one bound to be fatal, and the eggs
you avoided for years were not,
after all, the source of cholesterol.
To be happy, my friend, don't read
the newspapers, gossip, or go
where subliminal ads will entrap.

Tell me or don't. I'd rather not know.
Not long ago I had a few days
of serenity because I canceled
the papers, silenced the TV and radio.
But am I wise enough to sustain
such saintly transcendence? Do I not
feel obliged to be enraged and helpless?

But you ask about Hamlet, if it is true
that King Claudius got a bum rap
from a stepson not diagnosed in time
to prevent his hysterical crimes?
All I, your professor, can convey
is the latest scholars have found —
that Prince Hamlet was gay and bipolar,
and feigned madness to stay out

of a soon to explode Scandinavian war.

As for the wars undertaken in our time
I can only hazard a guess that the truth
is more to be found in the dust of Kabul
or Baghdad or in the face of a terrified
child than in any words mouthed by those
who would have you believe
the lies they would have you believe.

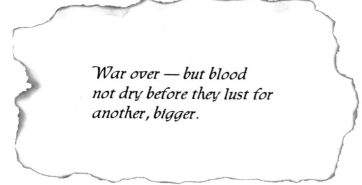

*War over — but blood
not dry before they lust for
another, bigger.*

UPDATE ON THE WAR
AGAINST LOVE ⋀⋎⋀

The President, when asked about gay marriage,
replies that he's aware that we're all sinners.
He must be referring to our disobedience
of the ten commandments, committing such acts
as murder, invading other nations, lying
and living a wholly deceitful life, polluting
the planet and robbing future generations
of their legacy in order to give to rich friends.

I'm sure he must mean that sort of thing,
rather than using his power and eloquence
to refute The New Testament with its insistence
that the greatest of virtues is charity, meaning love
without any qualification about whom to love.
I'm sure our President would not be casting
a malicious eye on loving men or loving women.

The Pope too feels a need to speak out,
and reminds us that the inability to overpopulate
the planet precludes gays and lesbians
from marriage. According to the Vatican,
"approval of deviant behavior" is a no-no
and adoption of children by same-sex couples
"would actually mean doing violence to these
children, putting them in unhealthy home
environments." Little, I suspect, do the framers
of this doctrine know how unloved children
feel as they languish in orphanages or wander
streets or are put to death one way or the other.

I myself have tried to love and even adopt
our President, as have so many who love him.
And I wish the Pope well, for I too suffer

from arthritis. Yet I often wonder why
in their ceaseless pondering of policies they
and their advisers never consider the option
expressed in the phrase Live and Let Live,
a doctrine that could apply to many situations,
including the choice of love over bombs and deceit.

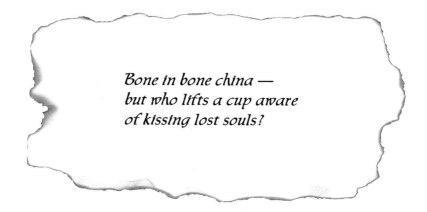

Bone in bone china —
but who lifts a cup aware
of kissing lost souls?

DINNER AT THE RANCH ⋏⋎⋏

The huge rising moon, gold as a doubloon,
is the only object in sight our host does not own.
And how fortunate are we who sit at his long table
under the shimmering stars and the satellites
that gaze down upon us like hawks sighting mice!

Our menu by morning will be news around the globe —
fare from a number of nations, sampled at least
by the Chief, though beef is still his prime choice,
as witnessed by bleached cow skulls impaled on fences.

Only I, a guest thanks to some error, think I hear
those skulls hum as they solicit the sky like the bones
of vanished Apaches. I would not be surprised
to see a brave appear and insist on having his say —

belated, yet still not too late for the record. Had dice
been thrown with a different flick of the White Father's
wrist, our host this evening might be Geronimo, not
The Great White Father's successor, and those string
beans dangling from the mesquite would have been
baked into bread for this banquet. After supper the Chief

spreads his blueprints. "We want to keep all my land
unspoiled," he tells us. He spreads his arms and turns
a full circle, taking in the panoramic horizon. His vision
includes a fence that will rise through the sky, higher by far
than the Great Wall of China — a shield of defense
for all time, and sure to keep out the terrible terrorists.

There's no need to consult wise men and women
regarding these plans — don't even suggest it. And by
the way, our host agrees with the N.R.A. that even

those terrorists have the right to purchase assault weapons.
The ethics of Western movies prevail, and therefore
lawmen never deny a black-hearted villain his right to bear arms.

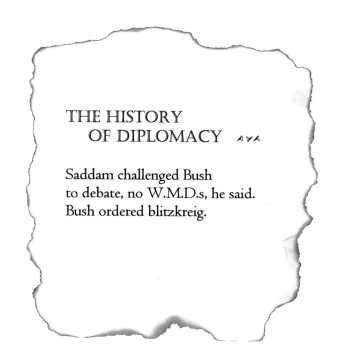

THE HISTORY
OF DIPLOMACY

Saddam challenged Bush
to debate, no W.M.D.s, he said.
Bush ordered blitzkreig.

JOURNAL ENTRY ▲▼▲

Once again mention of the war
ruined an evening. Up until then

it had been a delightful visit —
dinner, admiring the children,

sitting outside by the fountain,
praising the negative ions

that make us so happy. Perhaps
the secret of bliss is not speaking

of anything outside the walls.
I recall thinking that very thought

just before all hell broke loose,
for the war had snuck in like a snake

to spew its toxicity. "But we can't
just get out and leave them to chaos —

all hell would be sure to break out,"
says she, and he asks if it's not

already hell in Iraq and can we really
afford the billions and blood it takes

to convince these poor people they need
a nation like ours? "Bottom line,"

the honest host declares, "they've got
that oil and we've got to have it!"

ST. SEBASTIAN ▲▼▲

Since arrows came from so many angles
some may have pierced Sebastian before
he was tied up against an ornate column
of the hilltop ruins, and the arrow
that shot through his neck and exited
just above his eyes suggests that the archer
either crouched or was the size of a child.

The crossed or zigzag pattern of arrows
indicates at least two executioners
who must have been careful not to hit
each other, for friendly fire would
have been a risk with such a profusion
and some arrows must have gone astray
though the one that pierced Sebastian's heart
was a direct hit. The vane feathers almost
reach the blood oozing from the ribcage.

A pathologist could make sense of all this,
and might look beyond the tortured saint
to note how green and Edenic the earth
looks, as if only the ruined palace served
as the domain for such evil. The mountains
and fields and winding road are charming,
and the three archers trudging over a crest
in the distance look like hunters heading home.

Often overlooked in the blue sky is a cloud
bearing a horse and horseman over the scene,
for Andrea Mantegna seems to have thought
there is always a witness observing all
that takes place below, including Sebastian
and the archers bound for home with enough
pictures in their skulls to last a lifetime,
no need ever again for galleries or museums.

REFLECTION ⴽⵣⴽ

Our leader is a hollow man, they say,
wooden-headed, and not very bright,

misled by others who are Machiavellian,
while he is not. Yet he is the man

who gives orders, and when he does
many die, and they are just as dead

as if a great warrior has downed them.
But to the dead does it matter what manner

of fool or monster — charming or crude —
sent them their deaths, using weapons

fueled by enough propaganda to lift
great planes and missiles off the ground

and send them in graceful flight around the earth.

DEFINITIONS

I.

What is a war criminal?
Is it not a man
who lies to his people
and then declares a war
leading to the deaths
of hundreds, thousands —
more deaths guaranteed
down the years?

Is a war criminal
not a man who conspires
to invade another nation
on this excuse or that?
And if such a man is not
a war criminal, who is?

Pray tell me. Of course
you must exempt
the most obvious.

II.

What's in a phrase,
a saying, an image?

In Korea
"the ochre road"

leads from life
to death. Flying

into Los Angeles
I see a vast

ochre sky of smog,
truly a wide

road of death.
How many thousands

have taken it,
their breath rising

into the stratosphere,
all of us bound

to ochre, that road,
that cloud, that shroud of it,

be it here, be it there.

ASSUMPTIONS ▲▼▲

There is an assumption that a genial fellow
— as wooden-headed as any Barbara Tuchman
described in her great work, *The March Of Folly* —

is not capable of making a mistake
on a truly Hitlerian scale, even if he has
possession of far greater power and weaponry.

Some who fear his decisions call the man evil,
but others say that is giving him too much credit,
for most idiotic decisions come out of committee.

Tuchman knew that Der Führer adored opera
and Stalin diverted himself by playing Mozart,
so though comparisons are odious, our hope

may lie in the convergence of evil and high culture.

GOD'S LITTLE ACRE ▲▼▲

"Our grounds were neither auriferous nor
diamondiferous."
　　　Marie Cardinal, *The Words To Say It*

The Administration's chief adviser on global warming
is a scientist who does not believe it's a problem.

Even while interviewed he continues to sift dirt in his yard,
for he is obsessed with the conviction he'll find gold there.

In Erskine Caldwell's novel, *God's Little Acre,*
a Georgia geezer named Ty Ty had the same faith

and was always digging up his yard. One crater
after another appeared until his ground was so pocked

that his house was in danger of collapse. This belief
in auriferous soil must be some kind of archetype,

for Marie Cardinal wrote of her traumatic childhood
in France and how she spent her time seeking gold

or diamonds in the dirt and having to settle for pebbles.
"I scratched until it hurt," she wrote, "until I had

the sensation that my fingernails were coming off."
Like Ty Ty or the expert on global warming

or the President's men looking for weapons of mass
destruction the little girl Marie at last realized that all

she really wanted was a hug and kiss from father,
an insight that could banish the need for war.

PRAISING THE FOREST ᴧʏᴧ

The President's concerns are extensive.
You can almost feel him holding you
and yours in the light, Quaker fashion.

He cares about us all, and the land
we live in and the air we breathe
and the water we drink, and so on.

He has come to see the charred forest,
but it is reported that protesters line
the road up the mountain. Therefore

to avoid these impertinent citizens
the President is flown in a copter
from Air Force One, its engines

kept running to perfume the air
and in case a hasty exit is desired.
No one not an enthusiastic supporter

is allowed on the mountain to hear
his speech, therefore all their reports
are quite positive. In less than an hour

he has made his appearance and returned
to Air Force One, not to be late for
his fundraising appearance in Denver

and to give the latest report on his war.

BEFORE THE ELECTION ᴀ ᴠ ᴀ

*"What a noble epitaph, not to have conceded
at Olympia!"*
            — Greek boxer, 564 B.C.

"Platitudes have been my solution," she said,
"One day at a time!" and "Put one foot in front
of the other!" and "If you are wrong promptly

admit it and apologize!" But our President
is not in Alcoholic Anonymous nor tempted
to admit a mistake. In fact, he could not think

of even one when he was asked. No "character
defects" hath he. Then she said she was sorry
she could only clean up her side of the street

and only one short block of it at that. Those of us
who want to stop the war and banish those who
brought it upon the world would love to follow

the platitudes, but how can we? Cities in rubble
and faces of the fallen keep us awake while
the President, more popular than ever, sleeps soundly.

Those who have returned from battle in wheelchairs
or limp and shuffle about on prosthetic legs must learn
to live with platitudes, acquire the right attitudes.

But I have not that ability, for I still long to halt the war,
an attitude so naïve that even the so-called liberals
dare not mention that option lest they be banished.

COALITION OF THE WILLING ▲▼▲

*"But it makes me mad that this whole war was sold to the
American public and to the soldiers as something it wasn't."*
—Mother of Tristan N. Aitken,
killed in Iraq, April 4, 2003

When casualties approached one hundred
many said the war might become abhorrent,

but as losses climbed others were still gung ho,
and destroying distant cities seemed justified.

Our own were the only soldiers counted,
since vaporized Iraqis were consigned

to ashy air. A mother here or there complained
that her loss was all for naught, but her voice

was weak, unheeded, and her son or daughter,
after all, was only one — one body, one coffin,

one flag. Many despite their grievous losses
seemed proud to say the cause of this war

was just, regardless of why it was undertaken.
The President declared again and again

in his reelection bid that "Government should
improve our lives, not try to run them."

As coalitions of mice are easily led,
few have challenged his view that death

might improve on many a young life.

SEMANTICS ᴧᵛᴧ

My friend Elizabeth, a grey-haired
Quaker, is always asking questions.
This time she holds up a newspaper,
showing a photograph of the bodies
of children laid out in a row.
"Is it cowardly to do this," she asks,
      "bombing children like this?"

"They're the unintended consequences,"
I say, "They used to call them
collateral damage, but people got tired
of that term — I guess they saw too many
pictures like that one." I don't want
to look at it. In black and white
all toddlers look pretty much alike,
      much as mine used to.

"But is it *cowardly*?" she insists.
And again, I say it is a matter of semantics.
"Well," she says, "when they attacked
the Trade Center towers the President
and many others said they were *cowardly*.
Aren't our airmen doing
      the same sort of thing?"

She holds up the newspaper again.
And again I do not want to look at it,
but her look seems to demand an answer.
"It's just a matter of semantics," I say,
and wish she and I could be satisfied
      with sensible answers.

AN UNBROKEN CIRCLE ▲▼▲

"So men are smeared on the desert grass,
And the generals return empty-handed,
Know that weapons of war are utterly evil —"
—Li Po

For the two and a half hours
it took to read the names, each
given a toll of the bell,
they stood in a wide circle
at attention while the dust
swirled around like a dervish.

But where was the enchanter
and what did the whirlwind
mean to say? No one
had thought to damp down
the ground, mute the message,
calm the grit and ash so that grief

alone could command respect.
Though no one wished to think
of the bodies, but only of love,
they all breathed deep the sacred
molecules of blood and flesh
left for our legacy and eucharist.

A few held their breath as ash
whipped through the air,
but all who stood there partook
of communion, took in what
was left, just as after Hiroshima
and thousands of other disasters

there is always death in the waters,
earth, and air, bringing us back

those we thought to have left us.
We inhale them deep and they
drum on in our hearts, though neither
politician nor priest rises to speak
                                        of this.

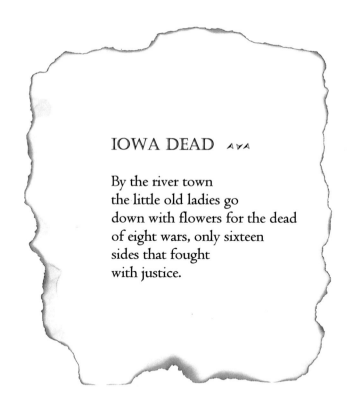

IOWA DEAD ᴀᴠᴀ

By the river town
the little old ladies go
down with flowers for the dead
of eight wars, only sixteen
sides that fought
with justice.

THE WHITE HOUSE
SCREENING ROOM △▽△

How many times did Dubya watch High Noon
then leave the screening room to rant more

about the need for action pre-emptive
for which no advice or approval was needed?

Like the Marshall prepared to face down
the three villains who threatened the town

our President would on the world stage
deal with the axis of evil. After all, Iraq

has dusty streets too, and if Gary Cooper
can clean up a town so can he, the President.

And no one had better stand in his way,
for in his heart he knows he is right.

He will win and stand tall and blow smoke
from the barrel of his pistol. In that same

screening room Nixon had watched George
C. Scott as General Patton with his pearl-handled

revolver as bombs fell on Cambodia, a secret
worthy of rape in the darkness. How many

have died because a President watched one
movie instead of another, acted out the scripts?

Reagan was so enthralled by the wisecracking
crew of a Flying Fortress returning from a raid

over Germany that he invented a whole mythic tale
and forgot he had only seen it in the screening room.

Perhaps in that magic place the real and unreal mate
and so entangle themselves in the minds of presidents

that monstrous births of events are inevitable,
inflicted on the world after the show or during inter-

mission when a call can order new horrors for those
who live in dusty streets of distant cities or in no homes at all.

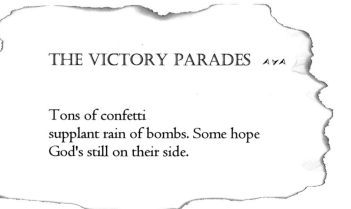

THE VICTORY PARADES ᴀᵥᴀ

Tons of confetti
supplant rain of bombs. Some hope
God's still on their side.

POPULATIONS ᴬᵛᴬ

As our van crammed with poets nudges
aside the mobs of Manhattan I reflect

that the population of Iraq is roughly
the same as that of New York City,

although a precisionist might add half
another borough, or say "plus or minus."

Imagine all that is being inflicted on Iraq
being done here, attacking these busy souls,

and how like one jigsaw puzzle piece
that obsesses, only Iraq — the size of just

one of our states — has become the be
and end all, with small regard for the whole

panorama. It is as if we are back to the wars
of city states, massacres like those on ancient

Aegean islands. But there I once found love,
and for a while forgot Armageddon.

THE LOST SOULS
FREE AS CRANES ⋏⋎⋏

A man's life sometimes goes on
after his soul has flown,
as fugitive as battered women.
And such souls never look back,
for they are happy to be freed
and know they are sure to find
better homes, all in due time.

Oh, it was not that he murdered
or encouraged others to do so -
Many a soul has borne that pain
when entrapped in great men,
and all earth's children must die.
What matter if it be of no
necessity but some man's will?

The skies are full of escaped souls
and it is a great mystery how
they manage to circle the earth
in such great numbers without
collision.   One may look up
to the more visible cranes
to observe such a wonder, see
how it's done. Meanwhile
the little men without souls
follow their strategies, predictable
as windup toys to anyone
who has a knowledge of even
one decade of ancient history.

FAR ABOVE
AND FARTHER ALONG ᴧᵛᴧ

"Farther along
we'll understand why."
— Gospel song

Find me the place in mid-air —
Sight it and point. Be not shy,
Show me where lost voices
Might yet be heard, and faces
Be glimpsed in the sky.

Have you not noticed in paintings
How some angels race after the others,
So eager to catch up? No more
Need than birds do our lost ones
Need steel or stone of towers that fell.

Nor do they require suburbs and subways,
Daily news of disasters and bombings
Or the new war born to serve vengeance.
Loved ones who remain often wish
They could have traded their lives,

But there is seldom a call for such sacrifice,
For the disappeared are free and on high.
And some who have reason to know
Say that angels frolic and play. If you
Look up you may manage to see them.

They look upon earth with no nostalgia
At all, find it tragic, amusing, appalling,
Smogged in, and they know that three
Or five acts are rare, though myth has it
Otherwise. And the dead keep the secret

That assassins succeed only in dreams.
Thus we must look beyond the day
That should not have been,
And pause now and then to love
One another, like angels and birds of the air.

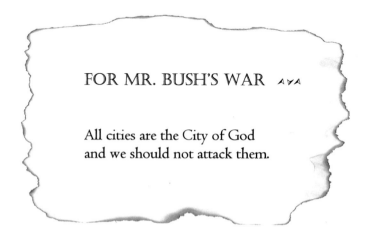

FOR MR. BUSH'S WAR

All cities are the City of God
and we should not attack them.

IN THE SAN DIEGO AIRPORT ᴀᵥᴀ

— for Samuel Ray and Dylan Annis

No shortage of babies today — I count
half a dozen and note that passengers —
a goodly percentage of them women —
are either pregnant or pushing strollers,
and several toddlers are running around
the carpeted areas, some being chased
by older siblings. A boy about two, nose
pressed to the glass, stands by his father
who is explaining that the plane almost
touching the window will soon take them
into the sky. "All the way up to heaven?"
the boy asks, and the father says, "No,
we come down when we get to Denver."

There is, it seems, no shortage of babies
though at least two are missing today
and these others are not nearly sufficient
replacements. It is small comfort that Sam
and Dylan seem to prosper in the arms
of parents more fortunate. But in truth
it is too much a struggle to wish them well
and rejoice in their good luck while we feel
we have none. That, we know, is an erroneous
reaction, an ungrateful response to the gifts.
Even clones of our lost ones we should love
as our own, but no god has taught us how.

There is no shortage of babies today,
at least in the San Diego airport, and yet
I am looking back to the great die-off
when all humanity shrank to the size
of a bottleneck, our numbers constricted

so that only the most hardy survived.
Inside trees and rocks the record is clear,
how humanity lived, how it died. A Samuel
here, a Dylan there, then both resurrected
in the arms of strangers. Others like us must,
wherever they travel, spot their lost ones, too,
as in today's airport so crowded with ghosts,
clones, and more than a few resurrected angels.

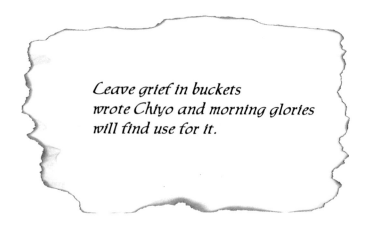

*Leave grief in buckets
wrote Chiyo and morning glories
will find use for it.*

ISSA'S DEWDROP ▲▼▲

the hole
will expand to consume every word we have uttered

what is left
when worlds blew apart and became us and cosmic dust

could prove
the gods had a murderous mandate right from the outset

the first word
and the last are as one, all flaws in the vast fabric combined

doomed
to become one giant hole — call it ether, call it space

call it a black
hole, and yet, Issa, you and I know there is no storm

like grief
for a child, then the leaden calm after. Call it forever

call it eternal
call it a dewdrop with a storm in it not named or numbered

though you and I
each bear a name like a scar on a heart black and blue

DAVID RAY's books include *Sam's Book, Wool Highways, The Mulberries of Mingo & Other Stories, Demons in the Diner, The Maharani's New Wall, Not Far from the River, The Endless Search,* a memoir, and *One Thousand Years: Poems About the Holocaust.* David has edited numerous anthologies. During his tenure as executive editor of *New Letters* magazine, he dramatically expanded the scope of the publication and launched the world renowned radio broadcast *New Letters on the Air.*

Even before the publication of David's first book, *X-Rays,* William Carlos Williams praised his work as "the best thing that's come out of any English department in fifty years." David is the only poet to have won the William Carlos Williams Award twice, and has won many other awards for fiction, poetry, and essays. With Robert Bly, David co-founded American Writers Against the Vietnam War in 1966 and they co-edited *A Poetry Reading Against the Vietnam War,* a collection of relevant readings from the classics as well as contemporary sources. He conducts readings and workshops, and can be reached at **www.davidraypoet.com.** **[PHOTO BY WILLIAM STAFFORD]**

HOWLING DOG PRESS
BRAVE NEW WORLD ORDER BOOKS
www.HowlingDogPress.com/Sardanapalus
ISBN: 1-882-863-55-0